"Myne Owne Ground"

"*Myne Owne Ground*"

Race and Freedom
on Virginia's Eastern Shore,
1640–1676

T. H. Breen
Stephen Innes

New York   Oxford
OXFORD UNIVERSITY PRESS
1980

Copyright © 1980 by Oxford University Press, Inc.

Library of Congress Cataloging in Publication Data

Breen, T. H.
  "Myne owne ground."

  Includes index.
    1. Afro-Americans—Virginia—Eastern Shore—History.
2. Eastern Shore, Va.—Race relations.   3. Eastern
Shore, Va.—History. I. Innes, Stephen, joint author.
II. Title.
F232.E2B73   975.5'1   80-12369
ISBN 0-19-502727-2

Printed in the United States of America

For
Susie M. Ames

Acknowledgments

While writing this book, we received encouragement and assistance from a great number of generous people. Rosemarie Zagarri helped us at an early stage of the research, and she provided many thoughtful suggestions for improving the project. Brooks Miles Barnes showed us important resources for the history of Virginia's Eastern Shore that we might otherwise have overlooked. The staff of the Virginia State Library, Richmond, was courteous and understanding, especially when we ordered Northampton County Court records through inter-library loan. Marjorie Carpenter of the Northwestern University Library patiently processed our requests for additional research materials. And the Northwestern University Research Committee awarded us several timely grants, one to cover research expenses and the other to have the manuscript typed.

Once we had written a full draft of the book, we prevailed upon colleagues and friends to read our work. Their criticism—constructive, detailed, and imaginative—proved of immense value not only in polishing our prose style, but also in developing new insights into the character of race relations in seventeenth-century Virginia. As much as possible, we attempted to incorporate their suggestions into the present volume, and we hope that these people are pleased with the final results: Josef J. Barton, Susan C. Breen, Thomas Durica, Stephen Foster, George M. Fredrickson, Elizabeth Haight, Susan Jacob, William A. Link, Charles W. McCurdy, Sharon H. McCurdy, Joseph Miller, Chester Pach, David Roediger, and Ella Wood. We especially thank the members of a National Endowment for the Humanities Seminar held at Northwestern University 1978–79 for their help: Thomas F. Armstrong, Gerry F. Moran, Mark A. Noll, Howard B. Rock, Philip J. Schwarz, Joel Shufro, and James Walsh. Sheldon Meyer of the Oxford University Press encouraged us when we most needed it, and Sarah H. Breen proofread the footnotes. Joe Rockey of Northwestern University drafted the map. Carrie Richgels prepared the index.

We reproduced spelling exactly as it appeared in the seventeenth-century sources. Wherever necessary we transposed "i" for "j," "u" for "v," "th" for "y," used a single form of "s," inserted appropriate punctuation, and expanded abbreviations to correspond to modern usage.

Finally, we want to explain the dedication. We never met Susie M. Ames; we wish we had had the opportunity to do so. Unfortunately, she died several years before we began our research. She was a scholar who obviously loved the Eastern Shore, and for half a century she wrote about the people who inhabited this region during the colonial period. Without her pioneering work—particularly her meticulous editing of the early county court records—we could not have produced this study.

April 1980   T. H. Breen
                                                            Stephen Innes

Contents

"Myne Owne Ground"

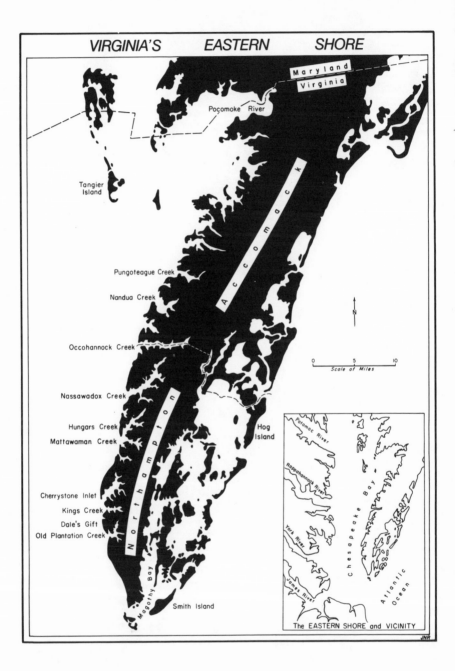

VIRGINIA'S EASTERN SHORE

Maryland
Virginia

Poçomoke River

Tangier
Island

A
c
c
o
m
a
c
k

Pungoteague Creek

Nandua Creek

Occohannock Creek

N

0   5   10
Scale of Miles

Nassawadox Creek

N
o
r
t
h
a
m
p
t
o
n

Hungars Creek
Mattawaman Creek

Hog
Island

Cherrystone Inlet
Kings Creek
Dale's Gift
Old Plantation Creek

Magothy Bay

Smith Island

Potomac River

Rappahannock River

York River

James River

Chesapeake Bay

Atlantic Ocean

The EASTERN SHORE and VICINITY

JNR

Introduction

Slavery is an American embarrassment. The nation's historic treatment of black men and women has compromised its perfectionist and egalitarian ideals. The American conflict between slavery and freedom has its roots in the seventeenth century. It was then that Europeans first displayed a dramatically heightened devotion to liberty in Europe itself while enthusiastically building a far-flung mercantile empire based on slave labor. As David B. Davis observes, despite the visionary expectations of many of North America's first colonizers, "Far from bringing a message of hope and redemption, America provided an unlimited field for the exploitation of man's fellow beings."[1]

We would be confronted with a considerable anomaly if some form of bonded labor had *not* taken root in early Virginia. Chattel slavery existed in every colony in the New World from Canada to Rio de la Plata. Men had been enslaving one another for over three thousand years, receiving philosophic justification from every major Western thinker from Plato to Locke.[2] Not until the mid-eighteenth century, with the emergence of Quaker abolitionist organizations, was sustained and coherent objection raised against the institution. The historian's task, therefore, is not to explain *why* slavery took hold in the English colonies, but rather to examine the particular evolutionary forms this labor system assumed in the West Indies, the Chesapeake, and the Carolinas. And to avoid parochialism, we must remember to view North American slavery fully within the context of the developing South Atlantic trading system.[3]

At its height the South Atlantic slave trade linked the four continents that face on the Atlantic Ocean. After a hesitant beginning in the late fifteenth century, the trade achieved its mature form by 1600. Europeans brought iron bars, textiles, firearms, and liquor to the western coasts of Africa, receiving consignments of slaves in return. The slaves were transported to Brazil, the Caribbean, and after 1640, to continental North America. The highly profitable tropical staples produced by this slave labor—sugar, tobacco, indigo, cotton—were then shipped back to European markets.[4] The slave trade peaked during the late eighteenth century, with annual volume figures exceeding seventy thousand in the 1780s, and it was not finally extinguished until the mid-nineteenth century—after over ten million people had been transported. The largest forced migration in human history, the slave trade involved the union of European capital and African labor in the newly colonized American tropics. The Atlantic slave trade drew on an African slave trade ancient in origins and it linked these small-scale, domestic, and variegated African forms of bondage with radically different large-scale plantation labor systems in the Americas.[5]

The arrival of black slaves in mid-seventeenth-century Virginia confronted English settlers with problems for which there were no obvious Old World solutions. First, slavery was moribund in England itself, and had been since the thirteenth century. Slavery remained on the English statute books in the institution of villenage, dating back to Roman times. However, during the period from the late fourteenth to the seventeenth century, personal feudal services gave way to impersonal rents, contractual obligations, and money payments. Villenage in practice became extinct in all but the remotest parts of England. Slavery, as a legal status, only occasionally received statutory implementation. A temporary law of 1547 mandated that beggars fleeing from enforced service were to be branded on the forehead with the letter "S," indicating that they would be "slaves" until death.[6] A second problem for the Virginia colonists resulted from their sense of cultural superiority, particularly as it related to vaguely racialist conceptions of the "genius" of the English people. This cultural chauvinism made it unlikely that the colonists would accept blacks *into* their society in any kind of participatory fashion. To accept massive numbers of people so profoundly alien to English traditions risked permanent disjunctions within the social order. Their unfamiliarity with the institution of slavery and their xenophobia presented the colonists with two equally undesirable alternatives. They could reintroduce the institution as the special and exclusive province for Africans and Indians, or they could attempt to moderate their cultural parochialism and bring blacks into their society after a period of apprenticeship as bonded laborers.

We know the tack they ultimately took. But, as this study reveals, the route to this decision was more circuitous than many have imagined. The process of black debasement and degradation was not linear and foreordained. As the following examination of free blacks in seventeenth-century Northampton County, Virginia, suggests, Englishmen and Africans could interact with one another on terms of relative equality for two generations. The possibility of a genuinely multiracial society became a reality during the years before Bacon's Rebellion in 1676. Not until the end of the seventeenth century was there an inexorable hardening of racial lines. We argue that it was not until the slave codes of 1705 that the tragic fate of Virginia's black population was finally sealed. An awareness of the awesomeness of this tragedy—for white and black alike—must not blind us to the variety of human relationships possible during the preceding eighty years. Only by maintaining sensitivity to the expectations and goals of the people who in fact lived in seventeenth-century Virginia—from their, not our own, vantage point—will we be able fully to understand this impending transformation.

The story of Northampton's free blacks is bittersweet. We trace the rise of remarkable men out of bondage into positions that brought them personal dignity and independence. For a brief moment it seemed, in one county, as if black Virginians would form a free peasantry capable of holding its own in a developing plantation society. But sometime during the third quarter of the seventeenth century the avenue to economic freedom closed. By 1700, people like the slave-holding black planter Anthony Johnson no longer appeared in the records, and the free blacks who took their places possessed what one historian has understandably termed "quasi freedom."[7] They were transformed, through processes which we shall examine, into objects of pity and scorn. They were people who had been used up and cast aside, persons driven to petty thievery in order to survive. Freedom for such marginal figures was desperately insecure and many probably did not regard it as a significant improvement over slavery.

Property made the difference. The black peasants of mid-century Northampton owned sizable tracts of land, competed with white neighbors in the marketplace, built up impressive herds of livestock, and from time to time, purchased dependent laborers. Property provided a livelihood as well as immunity from depredation. It gave them identity before the law and security in times of trouble. The county records contain many examples of the free blacks' spirited sense of their own liberty. Few, however, are so vivid as Edwyn Conaway's deposition taken in open court in 1645. Conaway, then clerk of the Northampton County court, reported that a man identified only as "Anthony the negro" and Captain Philip Taylor had gone out to view a cornfield in which both held an interest. Upon seeing them return, Conaway asked Anthony what had occurred, and the black farmer responded, "Mr. Taylor and I have devided our Corne And I am very glad of it [for] now I know myne owne, hee finds fault with mee that I doe not worke, but now I know myne owne ground and I will worke when I please and play when I please."[8] No Virginia yeoman could have stated the point more forcefully. Without the right to achieve the necessary conditions of liberty, to know one's "owne ground," freedom becomes a hollow concept, no less so in the twentieth century than it was in the seventeenth.

1

Patriarch
on Pungoteague Creek

Anthony Johnson would have been a success no matter where he lived. He possessed immense energy and ingenuity. His parents doubtless never imagined that their son would find himself a slave in a struggling, frontier settlement called Virginia. Over his original bondage, of course, Johnson had no control. He did not allow his low status in the New World to discourage him, however, and in his lifetime he managed to achieve that goal so illusive to immigrants of all races, the American dream. By the time Johnson died he had become a freeman, formed a large and secure family, built up a sizable estate, and in the words of one admiring historian, established himself as the "black patriarch" of Pungoteague Creek, a small inlet on the western side of Northampton County.[1]

Despite his well-documented accomplishments, Johnson has fared poorly in the hands of historians. For the most part, the reasons for this oversight are obvious. Before the American Revolution, Virginians paid scant attention to the colony's past. The seventeenth century seemed filled with failures, massacres, and stupidity, and even if Robert Beverley or William Stith had examined the manuscript records of Northampton County, they would not have found Johnson's story edifying.[2] At the end of the eighteenth century, Virginians invented a history filled with dashing cavaliers who, according to local legend, had been exiled to the Chesapeake for their loyalty to Charles I.[3] Again, there was no place for Johnson, a black man, in this nostalgic reconstruction. Anthony Johnson and his free black neighbors entered the historical literature early in the twentieth century. Unfortunately, their discovery occurred at a time of heightened race consciousness, and even the ablest scholars appeared perplexed by Johnson's economic success. Philip Alexander Bruce, for example, was a careful researcher, but his racial biases shaped his views of Johnson's activities. The Northampton colonist was one of "a number of persons of African blood in the Colony, who had raised themselves to a condition of moderate importance in the community."[4] Despite his condescending tone, Bruce alerted other historians to Johnson's existence. John H. Russell's *The Free Negro in Virginia 1619–1865*, first published in 1913, contained a more detailed, sensitive account of the Pungoteague blacks, but even Russell registered surprise at the size of Johnson's estate.[5] The experience of this particular black planter was juxtaposed against that of colonial slaves, and by that standard his accomplishments seemed strikingly anomalous, evidence to be explained away rather than investigated. Indeed, even in subsequent scholarship, Johnson remained something of an oddity. One of the more sympathetic treatments of his life concluded with the observation, "The question concerning the economic activities of the Negro inhabitants of Pungoteague and other Virginia communities is not one of major historical significance." Johnson rose from obscurity only to become a curiosity.[6]

Before relegating Johnson to historical miscellany, we should review exactly what is known about his life. A reinvestigation of this material serves several ends. First, it brings together scattered pieces of information about the Johnson family and therefore helps us to place specific events into the context of a long and complex life history. And second, by viewing this evidence from an ethnographic perspective, we discover that seemingly antiquarian reports and observations actually hold considerable cultural significance.[7] Johnson's experiences, in fact, demonstrate dramatically the interpretive problems facing the historian of race relations in mid-seventeenth-century Virginia.

Johnson arrived in Virginia sometime in 1621 aboard the *James*. People referred to him at this time simply as "Antonio a Negro," and the overseers of the Bennett or Warresquioake (Wariscoyack) plantation located on the south side of the James River purchased him to work in their tobacco fields.[8] In a general muster of the inhabitants of Virginia made in 1625, Anthony appeared as a "servant," and while some historians argue that many early blacks were indentured servants rather than slaves, Anthony seems to have been a slave.[9] Like other unfree blacks in seventeenth-century Virginia, he possessed no surname. Had he been able to document his conversion to Christianity—preferably by providing evidence of baptism—he might have sued for freedom, but there is no record that he attempted to do so. He settled on Bennett's plantation, no doubt more concerned about surviving from day to day than about his legal status.[10]

The 1620s in Virginia were a time of great expectations and even greater despair. The colony has been described as "the first American boom country," and so it was for a very few men with money and power enough to purchase gangs of dependent laborers.[11] For the servants and slaves, however, the colony was a hell. Young men, most of them in their teens, placed on isolated tobacco plantations, exposed constantly to early, possibly violent, death, and denied the comforts and security of family life because of the scarcity of women, seemed more like soldiers pressed into dangerous military service than agricultural workers. They would certainly have understood Lytton Strachey's poignant phrase, "the abridgment of hope."[12]

Immediately before Johnson arrived at Warresquioake, the Virginia Company of London launched an aggressive, albeit belated, program to turn a profit on its American holdings. Sir Edwin Sandys, the man who shaped company policy, dreamed of producing an impressive array of new commodities, silk and potash, iron and glass, and he persuaded wealthy Englishmen to finance his vision.[13] One such person was Edward Bennett, possibly a man of Puritan leanings, who won Sandys's affection by writing a timely treatise "touching the inconvenience that the importacon of Tobacco out of Spaine had brought into this land [England]."[14] Sandys dispatched thousands of settlers to the Chesapeake to work for the company, but favored individuals like Bennett received special patents to establish "particular plantations," semi-autonomous economic enterprises in which the adventurers risked their own capital for laborers and equipment and, in exchange, obtained a chance to collect immense returns. Bennett evidently sent his brother Robert and his nephew Richard to Virginia to oversee the family plantation.[15] At one time, the Bennetts owned or employed over sixty persons.

On Good Friday, March 22, 1622, the Indians of Tidewater Virginia put an end to Sandys's dream. In a carefully coordinated attack, they killed over three hundred and fifty colonists in a single morning. Fifty-two of these people fell at the Bennett plantation, and in the muster of 1625 only twelve servants were reported living at Warresquioake, which perhaps to erase the memory of the attack was now renamed Bennett's Welcome. One of the survivors was Anthony. Somehow he and four other men had managed to live through the Indian assault; the other seven individuals listed in 1625 had settled in Virginia after the Indian uprising.[16] Johnson revealed even at this early date one essential ingredient for success in Virginia: good luck. In 1622 the *Margrett and John* brought "Mary a Negro Woman" to Warresquioake. She was the only woman living at Bennett's plantation in 1625, and at some point—we do not know when—she became Anthony's wife.[17] He was a very fortunate man. Because of an exceedingly unequal sex ratio in early Virginia, few males, black or white, had the opportunity to form a family.[18] Mary bore Anthony at least four children, and still managed to outlive her husband by several years. In a society in which marriages were routinely broken by early death, Mary and Anthony lived together for over forty years.[19] The documents reveal little about the quality of their relationship, but one infers that they helped each other in myriad ways that we can never recapture. In 1653 Anthony Johnson and Mary "his wife" asked for tax relief from the Northampton County court. The local justices observed that the two blacks "have lived Inhabitants in Virginia (above thirty yeares)" and had achieved widespread respect for their "hard labor and known service." The interesting point is that both Mary and Anthony received recognition; both contributed to the life of their community.[20]

Johnson's movements between 1625 and 1650 remain a mystery. Court records from a later period provide tantalizing clues about his life during these years, but they are silent on how "Antonio a Negro" became Anthony Johnson. Presumably someone named Johnson helped Anthony and Mary to gain freedom, but the details of that agreement have been lost. In 1635 John Upton, living "in the county of Warresquioake," petitioned for 1,650 acres of land based on thirty-three headrights. Included on his list were "Antho, a negro, Mary, a negro."[21] While these two blacks were probably the Johnsons, we have no reason to conclude that they were still slaves in 1635. Men like Upton saved or purchased headrights until they could make a sizable claim, and the headrights for Anthony and Mary may have circulated in the area for a decade.

We do not know when or under what circumstances Johnson transferred to Northampton. His former master, Richard Bennett, developed complex ties with the Virginia Eastern Shore. Between 1652 and 1655 he spent a good deal of time there keeping watch on suspected royalists. Bennett's daughter Elizabeth married Edmund Scarborough's eldest son, Charles. The Scarboroughs were the dominant family in Northampton County, and by 1652 Charles had already patented 3,050 acres on Pungoteague Creek. Like his father, he became a leader in local and colony politics.[22] Bennett may have brought the Johnsons to Northampton and then, as governor, looked after their legal and economic interests. The Johnsons may even have named their son after Bennett. There is no firm evidence that this occurred, but it is curious that the Johnsons appeared in the Eastern Shore records at precisely the time that Bennett became a major political force in the area.

During the 1640s the Johnsons acquired a modest estate. Raising livestock provided a reliable source of income, and at mid-century, especially on the Eastern Shore, breeding cattle and hogs was as important to the local economy as growing tobacco. To judge by the extent of Johnson's livestock operations in the 1650s, he probably began to build up his herds during the 1640s.[23] In any case, in July 1651 Johnson claimed that 250 acres of land were due him for five headrights. The names listed in his petition were Thomas Bembrose, Peter Bughby, Anthony Cripps, John Gesorroro, and Richard Johnson.[24] Whether Anthony Johnson actually imported these five persons into the colony is impossible to ascertain. None of them, with the exception of Richard Johnson, his son, appeared in later Northampton tax lists. Like John Upton, Anthony may have purchased headright certificates from other planters.[25] Two hundred and fifty acres was a considerable piece of land by Eastern Shore standards, and though the great planters controlled far more acreage, many people owned smaller tracts or no land at all.[26] Johnson's 250 acres were located on Pungoteague Creek.

In Feburary 1653 Johnson's luck appeared to have run out. A fire destroyed much of his plantation. This event—the Northampton Court called it "an unfortunate fire"—set off in turn a complicated series of legal actions that sorely tested Anthony's standing within the Pungoteague community, and at one point even jeopardized much of his remaining property. The blaze itself had been devastating. After the county justices viewed the damage, they concluded that without some assistance the Johnsons would have difficulty in the "obtayneing of their Livelyhood," and when Anthony and Mary formally petitioned for relief, the court excused Mary and the Johnsons' two daughters from paying "Taxes and Charges in Northampton County for public use" for "their naturall lives." The court's decision represented an extraordinary concession. The reduction of annual taxes obviously helped Johnson to reestablish himself, and the fact that he was a "Negro" and so described during the proceedings seems to have played no discernible part in the deliberations of the local justices.[27] Moreover, the court did more than simply lighten the Johnsons' taxes. By specifically excusing the three black women from public levies, the justices made it clear that, for tax purposes at least, Mary and her daughters were the equals of any white woman in Northampton County. Taxes in seventeenth-century Virginia were assessed on people, not on land or livestock. The definition of a tithable—someone obliged to pay taxes—changed from time to time. In the 1620s the Burgesses had included "all those that worke in the grounde." The Virginia legislators apparently intended to exempt the wives of white planters. Such women, it was assumed, busied themselves with domestic chores and therefore, did not participate directly in income-producing activities. Indeed, it was commonly believed that only "wenches that are nasty, and beastly" would actually cultivate tobacco. Black women, alone, in other words, demeaned themselves by engaging in hard physical labor. In a 1645 act concerning tithables the colonial legislators declared: "And because there shall be no scruple or evasion who are and who are not tithable, It is resolved by this Grand Assembly, That *all negro men and women*, and all other men from the age of 16 to 60 shall be adjudged tithable."[28] Why the Northampton Court made a gratuitous exception to statute law is not clear. Perhaps the Johnsons' economic success coupled with their "hard labor and known service" pointed up the need for local discretion in enforcing racial boundaries.

Anthony Johnson's next court appearance came on October 8, 1653. This time his testimony "concerned a cowe" over which he and Lieutenant John Neale had had a difference of opinion. The court records unfortunately provide no information about the nature of the conflict. The Northampton justices ordered two men familiar with the affairs of Pungoteague Creek, Captain Samuel Gouldsmith and Robert Parker, to make an "examination and finall determination" of the case.[29] Since the Neales were a powerful family on the Eastern Shore, the decision of the justices reveals the high regard in which Johnson was held.[30] Had he been a less important person in that society, they might have immediately found for Neale. Of greater significance, however, was the involvement of Gouldsmith and Parker in Johnson's personal business. Neither of them was a great planter; but both were ambitious men, who apparently concluded after their investigation that Johnson's fire losses had left him vulnerable to outside harassment.[31]

A year after this litigation had been resolved, Captain Gouldsmith visited the Johnson plantation to pick up a hogshead of tobacco. Gouldsmith presumably expected nothing unusual to happen on this particular day. Like other white planters on the Eastern Shore, he carried on regular business transactions with Anthony Johnson. Gouldsmith was surprised, however, for soon after he arrived, "a Negro called John Casor" threw himself upon the merchant's mercy. He declared with seemingly no prompting that he was not a slave as Johnson claimed in public. He asserted that the Johnsons held him illegally and had done so for at least seven years. Casor insisted that he entered Virginia as an indentured servant, and that moreover he could verify his story. An astonished Johnson assured Gouldsmith that he had never seen the indenture. Whether Casor liked it or not, he was Johnson's "Negro for life."[32]

Robert Parker and his brother George took Casor's side in the dispute. They informed the now somewhat confused Gouldsmith that the black laborer had signed an indenture with a certain Mr. Sandys, who lived "on the other side of the Baye." Nothing further was said about Sandys, and he may have been invented conveniently to lend credibility to Casor's allegations. Whatever the truth was, Robert Parker led Casor off to his own farm, "under pretense that the said John Casor is a freeman," noting as he went that if Johnson resisted, Casor "would recover most of his Cows from him the said Johnson."[33]

The transfer involved a carefully calculated gamble. Parker was tampering with another man's laborer, a serious but not uncommon practice in mid-century Virginia. Like other enterprising tobacco planters, Parker needed fieldhands and he was not overly scrupulous about the means he used to obtain them. The House of Burgesses regularly passed statutes outlawing the harboring of runaway servants, explaining, no doubt with people like Parker in mind, that "complaints are at every quarter court exhibitted against divers persons who entertain and enter into covenants with runaway servants . . . to the great prejudice if not the utter undoeing of divers poor men."[34] Regardless of the letter of the law, Gouldsmith reported that Johnson "was in a great feare." In this crisis Anthony called a family conference and, after considerable discussion about the Parkers' threats, "Anthony Johnson's sonne-in-law, his wife and his owne twoe sonnes persuaded the old Negro Anthony Johnson to set the said John Casor free now."[35] The word "old" stands out in this passage. In seventeenth-century Virginia, few men lived long enough to be called old. When they did so, they enjoyed special status as "old planters" or "Antient Livers," people who were respected if for no other reason than they had managed to survive.[36]

This dramatic conference revealed the strong kinship ties that bound the Johnsons together. The group functioned as a modified extended family.[37] The members of each generation lived in separate homes, but in certain economic matters they worked as a unit. Indeed, they thought of themselves as a clan. The bonds between Anthony and his sons were especially important. In 1652 John Johnson patented 450 acres next to his father's lands. Two years later, Richard Johnson laid out a 100-acre tract adjacent to the holdings of his father and brother.[38] Both sons were married and had children of their own. In family government, Mary had a voice, as did the son-in-law, but as all the Johnsons understood, Anthony was the patriarch. The arguments advanced at the family meeting, however, impressed Anthony. Perhaps he was just an "old" man who had allowed anger to cloud his better judgment. In any case, he yielded as gracefully as possible to the wishes of the clan. In a formal statement he discharged "John Casor Negro from all service, claims and demands . . . And doe promise accordinge to the custome of servants to paye unto the Said John Casor corne and leather."[39] The inclusion of freedom dues gives us some sense of the extent of Johnson's fear. Colony law obliged a master to provide his indentured servants with certain items, usually food and clothes, at the end of their contracts, but it was a rare planter who paid the "custom of the country" without wringing some extra concession out of the servant.[40] Johnson, however, was in no position to haggle.

But the decision did not sit well with Johnson. After brooding over his misfortune for three and one-half months, Johnson asked the Northampton County court to punish Robert Parker for meddling with his slave and to reverse what now appeared a precipitant decision to free Casor. The strategy worked. On March 8, 1655, "complaint was this daye made to the Court by the humble petition of Anthony Johnson Negro; agt Mr. Robert Parker that he detayneth one Jno Casor a Negro the plaintiffs servant under pretense that the said Jno Casor is a free man." After "seriously consideringe and maturely weighinge" the evidence, including a deposition from Gouldsmith, the members of the court ruled that "the said Mr. Robert Parker most unjustly kept the said . . . Negro (Jno Casor) from his master Anthony Johnson . . . [and] the said Jno Casor Negro shall forthwith bee returned unto the service of his master Anthony Johnson." As a final vindication of Johnson's position, the justices ordered Parker to "make payment of all charges in the suite."[41] Johnson was elated. Casor was reenslaved and remained the property of the Johnson family. In the 1660s he accompanied the clan when it moved to Maryland. George Parker, who had taken an early interest in the controversy, managed to divorce himself from the last round of legal proceedings. His brother, Robert, of course, lost face. A few years later Robert returned to England, wiser perhaps but not richer for his experiences on the Eastern Shore.[42]

It is important to recognize the cultural significance of this case. Throughout the entire affair the various participants made assumptions not only about the social organization of Northampton County and their place within that organization but also about the value orientations of the other actors. This sort of gambling can be dangerous, as Casor discovered. He wagered that he could forge patronage links stronger than those which his master had built up over the years. In other words, he viewed the controversy largely in terms of patron-client relations. Johnson, however, was much more alert to the dynamics of the situation than was his slave. Anthony realized that he and the local justices shared certain basic beliefs about the sanctity of property before the law. None of the parties involved, not even Casor, questioned the legitimacy of slavery nor the propriety of a black man owning a black slave. Tensions were generated because of conflicting personal ambitions, because tough-minded individuals were testing their standing within the community. In this particular formal, limited sphere of interaction, the values of a free black slaveowner coincided with those of the white gentry. In other spheres of action—as we shall discover—this value congruence did not exist.[43] Johnson owed his victory to an accurate assessment of the appropriate actions within this particular institutional forum.

In the mid-1660s the Johnson clan moved north to Somerset County, Maryland.[44] The Johnsons, like many other people who left Virginia's Eastern Shore during this period, were in search of fresh, more productive land. As in the Casor affair, everyone in the family participated in the decision to relocate. None of the Johnsons remained at Pungoteague. In 1665 Anthony and Mary sold 200 acres to two planters, Morris Matthews and John Rowles. The remaining fifty acres were transferred to Richard, a gift that may have been intended to help their youngest son and his growing family establish themselves in Maryland. Whatever the motive, Richard soon sold the land, his buyer being none other than George Parker.[45] John Johnson, the eldest son, also went to Somerset. He had already acquired 450 acres in Northampton and thus, apparently did not require his parents' financial assistance. A paternity suit, however, clouded John's departure from Virginia. He fathered an illegitimate child, and the local authorities, fearful of having to maintain the young mother and child at public expense, placed John in custody, where he stayed until his wife, Susanna, petitioned for his release. John pledged good behavior and child support and hurried off to Maryland, where he resumed his successful career.[46]

For reasons that are unclear, the Johnsons closely coordinated their plans with those of Ann Toft and Randall Revell, two wealthy planters from Virginia's Eastern Shore.[47] When Toft and Revell arrived in Maryland, they claimed 2,350 acres and listed Anthony, Mary, and John Casor as headrights. Whatever the nature of this agreement may have been, the Johnsons remained free. Anthony leased a 300-acre plantation which he appropriately named "Tonies Vineyard." Within a short time, the family patriarch died, but Mary renegotiated the lease for ninety-nine years. For the use of the land she paid colony taxes and an annual rent of one ear of Indian corn.[48]

Anthony's death did not alter the structure of the family. John assumed his father's place at the head of the clan. He and Susanna had two children, John, junior, and Anthony. Richard named his boys Francis and Richard. In both families we see a self-conscious naming pattern that reflected the passing of patriarchal authority from one generation to the next. Another hint of the tight bonds that united the Johnsons was Mary's will written in 1672. She ordered that at her death three cows with calves be given to three of her grandchildren, Anthony, Francis, and Richard. She apparently assumed that John, junior, the patriarch's son, would do well enough without her livestock.[49] The Johnsons' financial situation remained secure. John increased his holdings. In one document he was described as a "planter," a sign that his property had brought him some economic standing within the community. One of his neighbors, a white man named Richard Ackworth, asked John to give testimony in a suit which Ackworth had filed against a white Marylander. The Somerset justices balked at first. They were reluctant to allow a black man to testify in legal proceedings involving whites, but when they discovered that John had been baptized and understood the meaning of an oath, they accepted his statement. Even Casor prospered in Maryland. He raised a few animals of his own, and in 1672 recorded a livestock brand "With the Said Marys Consent." [50] No doubt, Casor had learned an important lesson from his dealings with Anthony. Property, even a few cows or pigs, provided legal and social identity in this society; it confirmed individuality.

The story of the Johnson family concludes strangely. Around the turn of the century, the clan simply dropped out of the records. We have no explanation for the disappearance. Perhaps Anthony's grandchildren left Somerset in search of new opportunities. Perhaps as a result of social and demographic changes in the eighteenth century they lost their freedom. Or perhaps the records themselves are incomplete. All we know is that in 1677 John, junior, purchased a 44-acre tract which he significantly called "Angola." The last mention of this small Somerset plantation occurred in 1706 when John—a third-generation free black—died without heir. [51] And with the passing of "Angola" may have died the memory of Anthony's homeland, which he left a century earlier.

After reading the history of the Johnson family, one can understand why scholars have had such difficulty interpreting it. Traditional categories of analysis fail to comprehend the experiences of people like Anthony, Mary, and John Johnson. On one level, of course, it is tempting to view them as black Englishmen, migrants who adopted the culture of their white neighbors, who learned to handle complex legal procedures and market transactions, and who amassed estates that impressed even their contemporaries. From this perspective we can make sense out of Anthony's victory over Robert Parker in the Northampton County court. Indeed, once the surprise of discovering that Johnson owned a black slave has worn off, we realize that in matters of personal property Casor's race counted for very little. Anthony was in competition with white planters who regularly exploited laborers, black, red, and white, for immediate economic returns. In this world, Anthony more than held his own, and the story of the Pungoteague patriarch and his sons becomes an early chapter in the saga of Old World immigrants "making it" in America.

Somehow this analysis seems incomplete. Pieces of the puzzle remain unaccounted for, and we know from a growing body of historical literature that European and African migrants reacted creatively to their new environments, preserving some traditions, dropping others, but in all cases, resisting assimilation except on their own terms.[52] If the Johnsons were merely English colonists with black skins, then why did John, junior, name his small farm "Angola"? His action, admittedly a small shred of evidence, suggests the existence of a deeply rooted separate culture. Moreover, there is the family itself. The Johnsons formed extraordinarily close ties. The clan was composed entirely of black men and women, and while one might argue that the Johnsons were constrained by external social forces to marry people of their own race, they appear in their most intimate relations to have maintained a conscious black identity.

The Johnsons knew they were "different" from their white neighbors. Their origins, the exclusive monopoly of slave status for blacks (dramatized by Casor's case), the *ordinary* presumption against blacks testifying unless there were countervailing circumstances of a highly unusual nature, all underscored on a daily basis their continual deprivation. But within this circumscribed environment, as the Johnsons' story vividly suggests, possibilities for advancement existed in 1650 that by 1705 were only a memory.

2

*Race Relations
as Status and Process*

The status of black people in seventeenth-century Virginia has generated fierce debate among historians. In part, the intense interest in the subject, especially since World War II, resulted from contemporary concerns about race relations. The efforts of black Americans to achieve full equality inevitably raised questions about the origins of racial discrimination in this country, and scholars became curious whether the racist attitudes they encountered in their own society could be traced back to the first colonists. What exactly had been the relationship between black slavery and white prejudice? Which came first?[1] Since Virginia was the earliest English mainland colony to legalize bondage on the basis of race, it seemed logical that the records of this colony would provide the answers.

The general outline of the black experience in seventeenth-century Virginia has not been in dispute. The first migrants of African descent arrived in the colony late in August 1619. John Rolfe was the only colonist to record this event, and even he did not think the sale of "20. and odd Negroes" warranted more than a few lines in a long letter to London officials.[2] Over the next forty years, Virginia's black population grew slowly, and at mid-century it numbered only about three hundred. At the time of Bacon's Rebellion the figure stood slightly above two thousand, principally from Barbados and New Netherland. At no point before 1690 did blacks comprise more than a small fraction of the total population.

The relatively small number of blacks living in Virginia did not dampen subsequent controversy over their legal status. If in 1619 the House of Burgesses had defined the Negro's standing in law, the researcher's task would have been much easier. But the colonial legislature did not address such matters until the 1660s. Before that date some blacks were slaves for life. Others, however, appeared to have been indentured servants serving somewhat longer terms than did their white counterparts. Since Virginians employed words like "slave" and "servant" loosely, often to describe the nature of the work itself rather than its legal standing, historians had trouble documenting patterns of discrimination.[3] Oscar and Mary Handlin, for example, argued that blacks were treated essentially like white indentured servants. In other words, during the first half of the seventeenth century, status was only marginally a function of color.[4] Other historians, like Carl N. Degler, have insisted that the English settlers always viewed the blacks as lesser beings, and thus, their legal status "was worked out within a framework of discrimination."[5] The resolution of this interpretive difference seemed important during the great civil-rights battles of the 1950s and 1960s, for as Winthrop D. Jordan explained, "if whites and Negroes could share the same status of half freedom for forty years in the seventeenth century, why could they not share full freedom in the twentieth."[6]

The search for the colonial roots of present-day race problems yielded inconclusive results. Historians uncovered only a few documents that spoke directly to the question of the blacks' status before 1660. A small number of ambiguous examples appeared repeatedly in scholarly essays. By the time Jordan wrote his magisterial *White Over Black: America Attitudes Toward the Negro, 1550–1812* (1968), the debate over the legal status of early black Virginians suffered from inanition. Jordan stated what others had come to suspect, "For the crucial early years after 1619 there is simply not enough evidence to indicate with any certainty whether Negroes were treated like white servants or not." He concluded that prejudice and slavery reinforced one another over the seventeenth century, or as he phrased the point, the two elements "may have been equally cause and effect, constantly reacting upon each other, dynamically joining hands to hustle the Negro down the road to complete degradation."[7] The question of status had been settled, albeit indecisively, and interpreters of the black experience shifted their attention to more recent, certainly better documented periods of American history. In 1971 Wesley Frank Craven reviewed the literature on early seventeenth-century Virginia race relations and suggested, somewhat obliquely, that scholars may have placed their emphasis on the wrong topics. "I have been struck," Craven wrote, "by the thought that American historians have been so largely concerned with the question of the Negro's status, with the origins of the institution of slavery, as to be indifferent to other questions they might have investigated."[8] Craven did not explain what kinds of projects he had in mind. Perhaps he merely intended to spark a thorough reexamination of the assumptions about race and race relations that had reigned unchallenged for nearly twenty-five years.

Three aspects of the literature on the seventeenth century deserve special reconsideration: first, a teleological assumption that since black people have generally been ill-treated in our society, the colonial historian's primary responsibility is collecting early cases of discrimination in hopes of better understanding later more virulent forms of racism; second, a perception of race that regards a man's color as sufficient explanation for his values as well as behavior; and third, a tendency to substitute abstract, often lifeless categories such as slavery for the study of actual race relations. Certainly a successful recasting of the debate over the character of race relations in seventeenth-century Virginia must take these themes into account.

Let us turn initially to the problem of teleology. As we have already noted, contemporary historians sometimes assume that decisions made in early colonial times were directly responsible for current racial tensions in the United States. They take for granted an unilinear development from 1619 to the present, a long chain of unhappy events leading inevitably to chattel slavery, lynching, and institutional racism. Such a view of the past at least offers a convenient sorting device. If one knows in advance how the story will turn out, then one has little problem establishing a research design. Teleology provides direction, and the historian's job—whether he admits it or not—becomes one of busily collecting examples of racial discrimination. Lawyers call this approach the "leading case" method; Herbert Butterfield labeled an analogous approach the "Whig interpretation of history." In any form, it grossly simplifies causal links, making actual men and women living 300 years ago the servants of historical forces about which they possessed not the slightest knowledge.

The teleological interpretation becomes particularly obtrusive when we turn to the sparse records of early Virginia. It is not difficult to select laws from the colony's published statutes that specifically deny to black people rights enjoyed by whites. Someone with a sharp eye can even ferret out signs of racial discrimination long before the appearance of the first statutory references to slavery in the 1660s. The point here is not to assert that discrimination was insignificant in early Virginia or that the blacks were treated better than we imagined. Rather, we want to stress that there was nothing inevitable about the course of race relations, and when we study free black colonists within the context of their own society, we discover that they lived their lives, made personal decisions, and planned for the future in the belief that they could in fact shape their physical and social environment. If one misses this point and insists that these people were the victims of forces beyond their control, then one will not be able to make much sense out of the behavior of Northampton's free blacks.

A second assumption running through current writing on race relations is that in colonial times, if not in all of American history, blacks and whites formed solid, largely self-contained blocs. For obvious reasons this might be termed the monolithic perception of race. The literature contains many examples of this type of thinking. The very title of Jordan's *White Over Black* suggests the persistence of sharp racial boundaries over more than two centuries. And in a more recent, widely discussed publication, the racial categories are spelled out even more definitively. As A. Leon Higginbotham, Jr., explains in the introduction to *In the Matter of Color*, "In treating the first 200 years of black presence in America, this book will demonstrate how the entire legal apparatus was used by those with the power to do so [i.e., the whites] to establish a solid legal tradition for the absolute enslavement of blacks."[9] In studies like these, race itself becomes a sufficient cause for behavior. The logic, of course, is circular. White men and women think white thoughts and hold white prejudices because they are white. On the other hand, blacks subscribe to black thought patterns, and thus, once we know a person's skin color, we can explain his or her attitudes on a broad range of racially sensitive issues.

This form of argumentation creates considerable interpretive problems, not the least of which is that it flies in the face of social reality. To be sure, at a very high level of abstraction a scholar may generalize about the experiences of blacks and whites, treating them, in other words, as ideal types. However, the closer we examine specific biracial communities, either in the present or past, the more we discover that gross generalizations about race are misleading, if not altogether incorrect. We find ourselves confronted with too many exceptions, with blacks and whites who stubbornly refuse to behave as blacks and whites are supposed to behave. Sociologist William Julius Wilson recognized this difficulty and explained that "It is difficult to speak of a uniform black experience when the black population can be meaningfully stratified into groups." [10] The same case for differential behavior within a racial group can be advanced for whites. According to George M. Fredrickson, "Recent sociological investigations suggest that there is no simple cause-and-effect relationship between stereotyped opinions about a given group and discriminatory actions or policies. It is quite possible for an individual to have a generalized notion about members of another race or nationality that bears almost no relation to how he actually behaves when confronted with them." [11] Someone who understands the diversity of human responses to external factors will realize that certain activities—black slave-holding for example—do not need to be explained away as examples of social pathology.

Other factors besides race influenced the frequency and intensity of human interaction. Since whites and blacks came into regular contact throughout the colonial period, there is no legitimacy to the claim that each group developed cultural and social forms in relative isolation. As Herbert G. Gutman explained with specific reference to slaves, "The African slave learned much about New World cultures from those who first owned him, and the significant culture change that occurred between 1740 and 1780 has been obscured because so much of that interaction had been encased in snug and static historical opposites such as 'slave' and 'planter' or 'black' and 'white'." [12] Gutman's observation holds for the seventeenth century and for free blacks as well as slaves. At any given time, the character of race relations in early American was a function of *demography* (how many persons of each race were present in the society?), *spatiality* (how was the black and white population distributed over a region?), *ethnicity* (where exactly in Europe and Africa did these people originate?), and *wealth* (how did economic standing affect racial attitudes?). When one includes such elements in an analysis of a multiracial society like Northampton, one finds that allegedly sharp racial boundaries were actually blurred and constantly shifting.

Several examples taken from the historiography of seventeenth-century Virginia reveal the subtle—and sometimes not so subtle—ways in which the monolithic perception of race influences the scholar's imagination. We shall consider the value of colony law for the study of race relations, the controversy over arms and race, the problem of mixed racial groups of runaways, and finally, the manner in which the Northampton County clerk noted a person's race in the local records. First, there is the law itself. Historians have gained much of their knowledge about race relations in colonial times from statute law, in this case from William Waller Hening's collection of Virginia laws published early in the nineteenth century. A question immediately occurs about the limitations of this particular source. Presumably statutes passed in the House of Burgesses tell us something significant about perceptions of race in colonial Virginia. But what is it? Whose perceptions are reflected in the collected laws? If the answer is all "white" Virginians—and that is usually assumed to be the case—then the source most certainly has been misinterpreted.

When Winthrop Jordan wrote his book on American attitudes toward the Negro, he was keenly aware of this problem. He attempted to negotiate it by admitting that "while statutes usually speak falsely as to actual behavior, they afford probably the best single means of ascertaining what a society thinks behavior ought to be." He also noted that unlike the settlers in French, Spanish, and Portuguese colonies, "Englishmen had representative assemblies in America [which] makes it possible for the historian to ascertain communal attitudes."[13] In other words, English colonial society revealed its collective attitudes through the deliberations of representative assemblies. Since the particular political society or community we have been studying obviously did not include blacks, we must infer that the laws provide meaningful insight only into the white mind of Virginia. The problem here is that many whites were indentured servants, who were so unhappy about their condition in the New World that they regularly resisted the authority of their masters. In 1670, in fact, Governor William Berkeley and the members of the House of Burgesses became sufficiently worried about the unruliness of the colony's landless white freemen that they disfranchised them. Moreover, we know that blacks and whites cooperated under certain conditions—some even united in an attempt to overthrow the royal governor. While it is likely that poor whites and indentured servants shared the race prejudices of the great planters who actually wrote the laws, we cannot assume on the basis of statutes alone the existence of an undifferentiated white response to black Virginians.[14]

Clearly, assumptions about race solidarity have influenced our understanding of the blacks' right to bear arms. Historians recognize that a gun was an essential possession in seventeenth-century Virginia.[15] This was a violent society, and an unarmed black risked intimidation, if not physical harm, from aggressive whites as well as hostile Indians. A gun gave a man a sense of personal independence, a voice in local affairs that carried weight even when logic failed. It seemed self-evident to modern commentators that the House of Burgesses would not arm the members of an oppressed race. Unfortunately for curious scholars, Virginia lawmakers did not pay much attention to this issue before the 1660s. The only act in which Negroes and firearms were linked passed the legislature in 1640. It simply advised "all masters of families [to] . . . use their best endeavours for the firnishing of themselves and all those of their families wch shall be capable of arms (excepting negros) with arms both offensive and defensive."[16] Largely on the basis of this act, historians have drawn a number of conclusions about race relations in early Virginia. Moreover, the claims made for this particular piece of legislation have undergone a striking inflation over the last thirty years. Oscar and Mary Handlin gave only passing mention to the topic in their essay "Origins of the Southern Labor System," which first appeared in 1950.[17] After reviewing the Virginia laws, they found no evidence of a trend toward the systematic disarmament of blacks, and they did not even bother to quote the 1640 act. Carl Degler, however, disagreed with the Handlins' analysis. He argued that the arms law demonstrated how "Negroes and slaves were singled out for special status in the years before 1650."[18]

In an article published four years later, Winthrop Jordan decided that the statute was even more significant than Degler had thought. "Virginia law," he explained, "set Negroes apart . . . by denying them the important right and obligation to bear arms. Few restraints could indicate more clearly the denial to Negroes of membership in the white community."[19] In other words, this law provided important insight into the growth of white prejudice, and we can only infer that the possession of guns must have been a means of establishing well-defined racial boundaries. Degler later returned to the subject in a comparative study of race relations in Brazil and the United States. By this time, he had transformed the 1640 act from proscriptive legislation into a description of actual social practice.[20] The whites of Virginia owned guns; the blacks did not. We have moved in this escalating interpretation from a single,

somewhat ambiguous case of racial discrimination to a general statement about white attitudes toward all blacks and, finally, to a complete
disarmament of the colony's black population.

Considering the notoriety of the 1640 legislation, we should begin
our reassessment with the text of the law itself. Even a cursory reading
of the act reveals that the claims that have been made for it are unsup-
ported. There is no indication here, for example, of an effort by the
white colonists to disarm the black population, be they free or enslaved.
The legislation speaks specifically in terms of families. Masters are expected by a certain future date to have armed everyone "of their families" except Negroes. These black men presumably were slaves or indentured servants working on particular plantations. The law does not
prohibit a black master such as Anthony Johnson from possessing a
firearm, nor for that matter, does it order all blacks regardless of their
status to surrender their weapons to the state. And finally, the law does
not make it illegal for blacks to engage in offensive or defensive war-
fare.[21] It is true that the members of the House of Burgesses separated
some blacks out for special treatment, but little more can be said with
authority about the act. The Handlins were correct. The 1640 law
seems to have been an *ad hoc* decision related more directly to taxation
than to domestic security, and since the legislature did not raise the
question of the blacks' right to bear arms again for more than two decades, it does not appear warranted to interpret the act as strong evidence of white over black.

Examples drawn from different types of colonial records sustain
these suspicions. In July 1675 the Northampton County court issued a
warrant against William Harman, a successful free black farmer, "concerninge a Gunne found in the possession of the said Harman." A
white planter named William Grey had appeared before the local justices complaining that the firearm belonged to him. Harman insisted that
he had legally purchased the gun from Grey's wife, and after hearing
the evidence the members of the court found for Harman. The black
man kept the weapon, while an unhappy Grey paid court costs.[22] Nothing was said in this case about the defendant's race, and if we are
surprised by the Northampton judgment, it is probably because historians have misinterpreted the 1640 act rather than because black Virginians were actually disarmed.

The problems with the monolithic interpretation of race relations
become even more evident when we consider the active role that armed

blacks played during Bacon's Rebellion. Again, the failure to appreciate their participation in this political upheaval can be traced back to the 1640 legislation. Thomas Grantham, an English sea captain, arrived in Virginia just as the rebel forces were crumbling. Nathaniel Bacon had recently died, and apparently sensing an opportunity for easy glory, Grantham volunteered to negotiate in Governor Berkeley's name with several rebel bands that remained in the field. At the plantation of Colonel John West, supposedly the rebel army's "Chiefe Garrison and Magazine," the Captain found about four hundred "English and Negroes in Armes." Grantham no doubt exceeded his authority when he told "the negroes and Servants that they were all pardoned and freed from their Slavery." But despite the "faire promises" and despite a large quantity of brandy, "eighty Negroes and Twenty English . . . would not deliver their Arms."[23] Such figures reveal the danger of attempting to describe social practice on the basis of statute law.[24]

With hindsight the Governor's supporters may have wished that they had, in fact, disarmed the blacks in 1640. In an act entitled "Preventing Negroes Insurrections," the House of Burgesses in 1680 ordered that "it shall not be lawful for any negroe or other slave to carry or arme himselfe with any club, staffe, gunn, sword or any other weapon of defense or offence." The Virginia legislators made no reference to a failure to enforce the earlier law. And even in 1680, with the memory of armed blacks in open rebellion fresh in their minds, the Burgesses did not attempt to disarm *all* black men. The act specifically concerned "negroe slaves," and it does not appear that freemen such as William Harman ran much danger of being left weaponless.[25] Indeed, it was not until 1738 that the Virginia legislators declared that "all such free mulattos, negros, or Indians, as are or shall be listed [in the militia] . . . shall appear without arms."[26] By that time, of course, the social and demographic elements affecting the character of race relations had changed substantially, and the monolithic view of race may have corresponded to social reality more closely in this period than it did in the mid-seventeenth century.

The racially determinative interpretation of behavior has also affected our understanding of the ways in which Virginia courts punished runaway laborers. In the mid-seventeenth century, dependent workers—slaves and servants—frequently left their masters' service without permission. They did so for a variety of reasons. They resented the terrible work conditions, especially poor diet and clothing; stories of better opportunities in other colonies also lured them away. Since tobacco was a labor intensive crop and since good workers were both rare and expensive, the House of Burgesses devised ways to track down and punish servants who slipped away.[27] None of these controls was sufficient, however, to discourage desperate men and women from attempting to escape from the drudgery of plantation life. Sometimes blacks and whites ran away together, and when local authorities managed to recapture them, they meted out stiff punishments. The cases involving blacks and whites have played a major role in shaping our understanding of early American race relations. They have provided scholars with unusual situations in which persons of different races violated the same statutes. Historians have discovered that in general the court's treatment of offenders varied, depending on a person's skin color, the white runaways faring better than did the blacks. This has been interpreted as clear evidence of the white community's race prejudice, a deep-seated antipathy toward blacks that generated systematic discrimination long before the legislature got around to writing Negro slavery into law.[28]

Two cases adjudicated in 1640 have received particular attention. Because of their historiographical importance, we should consider them closely. In one case, three of Hugh Gwyn's servants appeared before a colony court. They had run away to Maryland, causing Gwyn considerable "loss and prejudice." The two white laborers, one a Scot and the other a Dutchman, were given thirty lashes, a harsh punishment even in seventeenth-century Virginia, as well as four years' extra service. The third man in this trio, "a negro named *John Punch*," received not only the "thirty stripes" but also was ordered to "serve his said master or his assigns for the time of his natural Life here or elsewhere."[29] As Carl Degler points out, Punch's treatment appears gratuitously severe.[30] The black endured the pain and embarrassment of a public whipping, but unlike the white culprits, he lost his freedom for life. "No white servant in America," Winthrop Jordan observed, "so far as is known, ever received a like sentence."[31]

The second case involved a complicated conspiracy. In July 1640 Captain William Pierce complained before open court that six of his servants and a Negro owned by a "Mr. Reginolds" had attempted to flee to "the *Dutch* plantation," presumably New Netherland. The group planned their escape with great care. The enterprise required courage, patience, and secrecy. The conspirators communicated between two plantations, gathered "corn powder and shot and guns," and then stole a skiff belonging to Pierce. They set off on a "Saturday night," and by the time they were apprehended they had sailed a considerable distance down the Elizabeth River. The chief organizer, a Dutchman named Christopher Miller, received the harshest punishment, a whipping, branding, shackling, and extended service. The other five white servants were given somewhat milder sentences, but they too suffered terribly for their bid for freedom. "Emanuel the Negro" was given thirty stripes, a letter "R' burnt into his cheek, and shackling for at least a year—all things which had been inflicted upon his co-conspirators as well. Unlike the whites, however, Emanuel did not have to serve extra time.[32] Degler argues, no doubt correctly, that the black runaway "was already serving his master for a life-time—i.e., he was a slave."[33] The court's actions demonstrated that some colonists, simply because of the color of their skins, found themselves reduced to a status below that of any white Virginian.

This analysis is persuasive to a point. Court decisions inform us about the interests and beliefs of the colony's white leaders, those planters who by 1640 owned large gangs of dependent laborers. Unfortunately, in their attempt to document the growing separation of the races, historians have ignored the highly instructive interracial cooperation to which these cases also speak. The conspiracy of the Elizabeth River servants is a good example of a much overlooked form of race relations. No one in Virginia regarded the crime of running away lightly. The chances of failure were great, and the seven laborers must have known that they risked extraordinarily severe punishments. Certainly, they could expect no compassion, for as the court explained, they had created "a dangerous precident for the future time."[34] The conspirators trusted one another. They had no other choice. Without secrecy, the project was doomed, and so far as the six whites were concerned, it did not much matter if Emanuel was black so long as he faithfully executed his instructions.

The need for cooperation increased once the group set out on its journey. The laborers had lived in the colony only a short time, and their knowledge of the winds and currents was consequently limited. The irresponsibility of any man placed the lives of all in jeopardy. The importance of strong personal ties would not have been reduced if these runaways had taken to the woods, where Indians waited to capture or kill the fugitives. Moreover, if the workers did not husband their provisions well, they could starve.

Despite these formidable obstacles, blacks and whites persisted in running away together. In 1661 the House of Burgesses attempted to stop these joint ventures by ordering "That in case any English servant shall run away in company with any negroes who are incapable of making satisfaction by addition of time [i.e., slaves], *Bee itt enacted* that the English so running away in company with them shall serve for the time of the said negroes absence as they are to do for their owne."[35] There is no evidence that this legislation was an effective deterrent. The possibility of large-scale, interracial cooperation continued to worry the leaders of Virginia. When a group of fugitive slaves frustrated all attempts to retake them in 1672, the planters' greatest concern was that "other negroes, Indians or servants . . . [might] fly forth and joyne with them."[36] These cases, of course, reveal only extreme actions, desperate attempts to escape, but for every group of mixed runaways who came before the courts there were doubtless many more poor whites and blacks who cooperated in smaller, less daring ways on the plantation. These forms of interaction did not mean that white servants such as Christopher Miller necessarily regarded Negroes as their equals, nor for that matter, that Emanuel thought any better of Miller because he was white. The low legal status of an Emanuel or John Punch, however, did not preclude their forging close relationships with certain white colonists.[37]

A final example taken from the records of the Northampton County court reveals how thoroughly modern perceptions of race solidarity have permeated our understanding of black and white in seventeenth-century Virginia. As we have seen, researchers using these and similar documents from other parts of the colony have collected cases in which a clerk jotted next to a man or woman's name the word "Negro."[38] Without such racial indicators, it would be virtually impossible for scholars to write about race relations. Indeed, it is only because of this assistance that we know for certain that a John Punch or an Anthony Johnson was black. No doubt, because the term "Negro" appeared so regularly throughout the pages of various colony and local records, historians assumed that seventeenth-century clerks were racists. No one stated the point quite so baldly, but they obviously believed that

Virginia officials classified people chiefly in terms of race. And thus, if a name appeared on a tax list or in a court proceeding without clear racial designation, one stated with a high degree of confidence that the person in question was white. It was difficult for the historian to imagine that in a society supposedly so anxious about setting the blacks apart from the whites any other system of record keeping would have been in operation. The problem with this racial logic is that in Northampton at least, the clerks did not always conduct their affairs by twentieth-century rules. Sometimes they carefully inserted "Negro" near an individual's name, but often, they simply recorded a person's identity without a racial tag. Perhaps the clerks were lazy; perhaps they regarded it a waste of time to write out "Negro" when everyone in the county knew full well that William Harman and Francis Payne were blacks? Or perhaps, they were not as racially conscious as some have surmised. Whatever their reasoning, many routine items—the sale of land and livestock, for example—did not carry the convenient racial indicators. Once the historian realizes that certain men and women were black, even when they were not so described, he can follow their lives more fully, studying economic transactions as well as the sexual and criminal activities that presently occupy a disproportionate place in the analysis of early American race relations.

A third general problem in the literature on race relations in colonial Virginia requires only brief mention. There is a tendency in some recent studies to substitute classificatory categories for real human beings. The reasons for this are complex. Such a strategy clearly lends itself to certain types of quantitative analysis, but whatever the justification, it usually leaves one with a sense that one knows a great deal more about an abstract category—slavery, the family, the plantation—and not much about the cultural and social interdependencies that gave meaning to people's lives. We may read at length, for example, about the institutional development of slavery without ever learning how specific, often idiosyncratic, patterns of master-slave relations shaped the planter's world as well as that of the dependent laborer. It is the human content of social arrangements that helps us to understand in what ways Carribean slavery differed from that of the Chesapeake, or how nineteenth-century Virginia slavery contrasted with that of the seventeenth-century colony. These observations about the contextual definition of slavery obviously hold for the free blacks. Freedom, like slavery, acquired social meaning not through statute law or intellectual treatises, but through countless human transactions that first defined and then redefined the limits of that condition.

II

This book focuses upon the lives of a particularly well-documented group, the free blacks of Northampton County. Even from this somewhat narrow perspective, we can explore general patterns of race relations and in so doing present ways of avoiding the interpretive problems that we have discussed in this chapter. In our attempt to pursue Professor Craven's suggestion that historians should push beyond questions of social and institutional status, we have made two assumptions. First, we regard race relations in this county—indeed, in all human relations—as a process, a series of personal interactions which in themselves generate meaningful definitions of status. It is the actual participants who do the defining and, as we have already seen, formal laws may or may not reflect the character of these continuing exchanges. A second, closely related point is that social groups, regardless of racial or ethnic composition, should whenever possible be studied within the context of the society of which they were a part.[39] An analysis of Northampton's free blacks, for example, without reference to other people with whom they came into regular contact would miss the complicated and creative methods by which these men and women shaped their world through interaction with persons of a different race and economic standing. The nature of our approach will become clearer as we examine specific evidence from the Eastern Shore. At this point, however, we should note the kinds of questions that we asked of the Northampton documents. Instead of searching for the origins of slavery or racism, we inquired into the ways the free blacks dealt with the local gentry; with middling white people; with slaves; with free blacks in Northampton? What was the purpose of these different types of interaction? What economic, environmental, and social conditions helped to determine the character and intensity of various personal exchanges?

After the passage of more than three centuries, we cannot recapture the varieties of behavior that one expects to find in the work of a good ethnographer. Nevertheless, we can speculate about the conditions that contributed to the formation of interdependencies, when, for example, economic and familial considerations weighed more heavily in a relationship than did color. Certainly, face-to-face contacts in seventeenth-century Virginia were not random. They involved choice. Within the constraints of custom and environment, people selected forms of behavior appropriate for various social transactions. In some relations, one or both participants regarded it as expedient to underarticulate his own culture. Compromises like these facilitated communication; they furthered social tranquility. Under other conditions, the same persons overstated their values. As anthropologist Fredrik Barth explains, "agreement on a definition of the situation must be established and maintained to distinguish which of the participants' many statuses should form the basis for their interaction. The process of maintaining this agreement is one of skewed communication: *over*-communicating that which confirms the relevant status positions and relationships, and *under*-communicating that which is discrepant."[40] In this sense, the forms of interaction (and race relations) were situational. They were defined within specific social settings, and while a certain type of relationship may have been associated in the participant's mind with an institution such as the church or court, the differential articulation of culture was usually highly personal and non-institutional in character.

Social transactions took place on three distinct levels. In mid-century Northampton free blacks and whites entered into patron-client relationships. Anthropologists refer to these arrangements as "lop-sided friendships" because the two parties involved possess unequal influence, status, or wealth. The nature of patron-client relationships varies from society to society, but several generalizations seem universally valid. However unequal the patron and client may be, maintenance of their relationship requires reciprocity. On his part, the patron—sometimes termed a broker or gatekeeper—provides the client with access to distant markets, with information about the outside world, with protection from external, largely impersonal government demands, and with advocacy in local legal proceedings. The client often has few material goods to offer in return. Nonetheless, he is expected to support the patron, perhaps through public displays of deference or vociferous political backing.[41]

With reference to seventeenth-century Northampton, two aspects of these arrangements merit special attention. First, virtually all free colonists—even prominent members of the gentry—stood as clients to someone. In the case of the great planter, the patron might be the royal governor of Virginia or a powerful London merchant. The various groups within this county community, like those in some contemporary Latin American countries, formed complex chains of dependency reaching from the center of metropolitan authority to the homes of peasant farmers.[42] Second, for the patron-client relationship to function smoothly, the broker must deliver the services that his clients expect. If he fails them, then the bonds of the personal contract dissolve and the clients seek out as best they can another and more reliable advocate. On the other hand, the client must be able to hold up his side of the bargain no matter how modest his efforts might appear.

The second sphere of interaction—at least, so far as the free blacks were concerned—involved family members and intimate friends. It is essential to see that this level of activity existed completely separate from patron-client relationships. Dealings within this second sphere were at once more intense and more informal than those associated with patrons and clients. Family and friends, of course, provided love, fulfillment, recreation, and security. While the forms of these personal contacts sometimes involved trade, the sale of a horse or pig, they were not primarily economic in character. On this level of human transaction, free blacks appear to have sought out other free blacks. In other words, racial identity figured much more importantly in this sphere than it did in the vertical exchanges with brokers. Possibly, common ethnic background as well as color increased the cohesiveness of the Northampton free black community. We shall speculate about the nature of these bonds more fully in a later chapter.

The importance of the distinction between these two spheres of activity becomes clearer when we consider the continuing scholarly debate over the survival of African culture in the New World. Until quite recently, researchers tended to interpret the survival of African customs as a dichotomous phenomenon, *either* black migrants preserved fragments of an Old World culture more or less intact *or* they lost meaningful contact with African folkways, imitating as best they could the culture of their white masters. From our point of view, of course, such a sharp distinction is artificial. When the free blacks we studied dealt with patrons, for example, they adopted forms of behavior suitable for that particular transaction. They dealt with leading planters in terms that the white colonists understood. In this sphere the free blacks attempted to transform themselves into black Englishmen; they purposely underarticulated whatever differences may in fact have separated them from other settlers. But within the second sphere, the same black man or woman may have expressed African values more forthrightly. These people were not behaving in a schizophrenic or disingenuous manner. Rather, within various spheres of experience they responded creatively to situational demands. [43] We would not assume, therefore, that a man like Anthony Johnson was necessarily out of touch with African values simply because he became a successful planter in a white-dominated society.

On a third level, the Northampton free blacks formed relationships with white indentured servants, poor to middling white freemen, and local Indians. Transactions with members of these groups varied in character to some degree, but in general, they were *ad hoc*, casual and ephemeral. Men exchanged goods and services for convenience and did not thereby establish reciprocal obligations. While these contacts were seldom dramatic, they revealed much about the extent of the free blacks' economic liberty at mid-century. Particularly interesting was the spatial dimension of the relationships that were formed within this third sphere.

Each sphere of interaction was equally important in the lives of the Northampton free blacks. It would be a mistake, therefore, to perceive this model as a series of concentric circles, the inner ring representing intense interaction among kin and close friends, and each additional circle depicting different and presumably less significant kinds of relationships. In point of fact, the spheres merged; they complemented each other. [44] Contacts with brokers, for example, were sources of economic and legal security that allowed this particular group of black Virginians to make decisions about family and friends without unusual fear of interference. This interweaving of transactional networks lay at the heart of the Anthony Johnson story. He recognized that well-developed ties with the members of the Northampton County court gave him strength and independence. Johnson and his family conducted private business as they saw fit. In the achievement and maintenance of a distinct social identity, the spheres played mutual roles.

3

Northampton County
at Mid-Century

The achievement of a small group of free blacks in carving out a relatively secure niche within Northampton's particular social environment
is remarkable, since by the middle of the seventeenth century, they had
almost nothing working in their favor. They succeeded in a frenetic,
competitive social system in which most men and women died young,
in which people had to be physically and mentally tough simply to stay
alive, and in which the rewards for the struggle were often sparse. To be
sure, some persons realized their dreams of property accumulation, but
for every great planter, hundreds of migrants experienced frustration and
pain. In the world of Northampton's free blacks, power usually meant
the ability to exploit the weak for profit, and though the county community contained sensitive, compassionate people, newcomers swiftly
learned that they had to look out for their own survival. It does not
require great imagination to realize that a poor or unfree person, especially a black one, faced very limited prospects on the Eastern Shore.
To appreciate fully the free blacks' accomplishment—described in detail
in Chapter 4—it is necessary first to comprehend the specific physical
and social environment in which they lived.

II

Physical environment played a central role in the lives of the seventeenth-century Virginians located on the Eastern Shore. Unlike those

settlers who established plantations far up the James and the York, well beyond the reach of salt water, the early inhabitants of Northampton County could not escape the omnipresent influence of the sea.[1] They were, for the most part, small-scale producers of grain, tobacco, and livestock, but their lives were bound up as closely with the annual rhythms of the Chesapeake as they were with the fertility of the soil. The sea shaped social and economic patterns in peculiar ways. The Chesapeake Bay—at least, the dozen or so miles of open water that separated the Eastern Shore from "the great Land"—assured the planters of Northampton a certain measure of independence from the government at Jamestown, but at the same time, political freedom allowed what Elizabethans called "over-mighty subjects" to exercise extraordinary control over their neighbors.[2] Moreover, the location of the county afforded direct access to world markets, yet as soon became apparent, Northampton lacked adequate deep-water ports to take advantage of this opportunity. Low-lying, sandy barrier islands gird the Atlantic Ocean side of Virginia's Eastern Shore. One, located near the entrance to the Bay, still bears the name of Captain John Smith, who explored this area during the summer of 1608. Others were named by the local Indians or by seventeenth-century colonists. Hog Island served an obvious function.

A glance at Augustine Herrman's 1670 map of Virginia reveals the Atlantic coastline in colonial times to have been quite different from the coastline today. Fierce winter storms and late summer hurricanes eroded the shore, and no doubt entire islands simply washed away. A man shipwrecked on one of these islands in 1648 left a vivid account of the weather: "The northerly wind that in these climates does blow very cold in the heat of summer, does much more distemper the air in the winter season . . . and did send so cold a gale upon the surface of the water in the creek I was to pass [a distance of only one hundred yards to the mainland], that, in the general opinion of all those concern'd, it was not a thing to be attempted; and if I did, I must surely perish in the act."[3] Not surprisingly, most early Northampton settlers set up their plantations on the more protected Bay side of the peninsula.

Quite different geological forces sculptured Northampton's western shore. Scores of creeks, all emptying into the Bay, created a multiplicity of small coves that defined settlement patterns. Some streams such as Old Plantation Creek and Kings Creek were named—or, more accurately, renamed—by the colonists, but a surprisingly large number of creeks retained their original Indian names, Mattawaman Creek, Nassawadox Creek, Occohannock Creek, and Pungoteague Creek, to name just a few[4] (see map). Early English explorers entertained high expectations for the streams of the Eastern Shore. They anticipated not only that the coves afforded safe, deep-water harbors, but also that the creeks provided easy access to distant inland resources. Such dreams, however, were quickly dashed. Captain Smith described the region as generally pleasant, with "some small creeks; good Harbours for small Barks, but not for Ships."[5] Captain Samuel Argall arrived at the same conclusion in 1613. Reporting on his visit to the Eastern Shore, he noted, "I found [it] to have many small Rivers . . . and very good harbours for Boats and Barges, but not for ships of any great burthen."[6] These observations were recorded before Virginians discovered the commercial value of tobacco. Over the long term, the shallowness of Northampton's creeks had a profound effect upon the local economy. It placed Eastern Shore planters at a competitive disadvantage in relation to the major growers along the James and the York. Ocean vessels could sail far up these rivers, take on cargoes of heavy hogsheads at plantation wharves, and while so doing have their hulls cleaned of sea worms by the flow of fresh water. But along the Eastern Shore, shoals hindered trade with ships heavier than seventy or eighty tons, and a tobacco planter living on a cove was forced to work out a difficult and often dangerous system of transfer from small shallops to trans-Atlantic traders.[7] Misunderstandings were common. In 1640 a furious controversy involving a ship captain who had waited "three dayes" off the Eastern Shore for a local planter who failed to appear at the appointed time had to be resolved by the Northampton court.[8] Unfortunately, there was nothing that the residents of the county could do about these navigational problems. In 1677 a group of them sadly noted "our Shore is Incompassed with Shoales Insomuch that no Ships but of small burden can com to Trade and those that com but few and Inconsiderable."[9]

Shipping hazards notwithstanding, Northampton County manifestly possessed considerable economic resources. The Virginia portion of the Eastern Shore was of low elevation, and while an imaginative observer may have been able to discern small hills, the area seldom rose to more than fifty feet above sea level.[10] The flat topography allowed Atlantic breezes to circulate freely. The climate was generally comfortable, the temperature ranging from an average winter low of 40°F to a summer high of 75°F.[11] English colonists who had experienced the stifling humidity of Jamestown appreciated the coolness of the Eastern Shore. The land itself supported a diverse and prosperous agriculture. Captain Smith praised Northampton's "pleasant fertile clay," soil that modern analysts classify as a fine sandy loam.[12] At mid-century Colonel Henry Norwood wrote that "*Northampton* county . . . is the only county on that side of the bay belonging to the colony of *Virginia*, and is the best of the whole for all sorts of necessaries for human life." Norwood did not describe these "necessaries" in detail; presumably he referred to the fine foods which the local planters set out for this English visitor.[13] The growing season lasted well over six months, and since the county received a substantial annual rainfall, Northampton farmers found no difficulty in producing good crops of corn and tobacco. The marshes and forests provided livestock with abundant feed.[14] In 1650 there were still enough large oak, hickory, and pine trees standing in Northampton to supply ship builders with beams and masts.[15] Even in the colonial period the abundance of waterfowl that wintered on the Eastern Shore impressed travelers, and in one case at least, migrant seabirds saved a group of shipwrecked Englishmen from certain starvation.[16]

For much of the seventeenth century, tobacco was Northampton's major export. In 1664 Eastern Shore planters "made" 1,622 hogheads of tobacco, about 8 percent of the colony's entire production for that year. Over the next two decades the region dropped behind Virginia's other counties in tobacco production, reaching a low of 4.2 percent of the total harvest in 1687.[17] These figures reveal an extraordinarily important shift on the Eastern Shore to other crops, and by the end of the century the transition from tobacco to cereals and livestock was almost complete.[18] In 1695 one person reported that "in some places on the Eastern Shore they plant no tobacco, not finding a market for what they have."[19] Even in the earliest days of settlement the agriculture of Northampton was probably more diversified than that of the James River counties, and this balance not only freed Eastern Shore farmers from a dependence upon a single staple commodity but also discouraged to some extent the development of large labor-intensive plantations. In this area, small grain and livestock producers, white as well as black, could participate profitably in the local economy.

The problem with the area—one that became more obvious over the course of the century—was Northampton's inadequate land base. This factor placed severe limitations on economic growth. The Virginia

Eastern Shore contained about 900 square miles, but much of this land proved unsuitable for cultivation. The average width of the county was only seven miles, and even the Accomack Indians who greeted the first English explorers recognized certain disadvantages connected with the environment. According to Laughing King, the "land is not two daies journy over in the broadest place, but in some places a man may goe in halfe a day, betwixt the Bay and the maine Ocean . . . so that by the narrownesse of the Land there is not many Deere."[20] The colonists, of course, made different demands upon the land than did the Native Americans. The early white settlers found sufficient acreage for their agricultural pursuits, but as the population grew, it was inevitable that families would push north in search of fresh land. Even as early as the mid-seventeenth century, aggressive Northampton planters clashed with Lord Baltimore's government over land that the Virginians coveted within Maryland.[21]

Northampton's physical environment, especially the separation from the main part of Virginia, was instrumental in shaping political and social relationships. Within the county itself people dispersed along the coves and inlets of the Chesapeake Bay and, because of the many obstacles confronting the seventeenth-century traveler, contact between scattered Eastern Shore families was sporadic. The Northampton court appointed highway surveyors, who proved spectacularly ineffectual in the task of creating reliable roads. In 1648 Colonel Norwood complained, "We were not gone far till the fatigue and tediousness of the journey discovered itself in the many creeks we were forc'd to head, and swamps to pass (like *Irish* bogs) which made the way at least double what it would have amounted to in a strait line."[22] Foot travelers who waited for ferries to take them across the creeks and rivers often made no faster progress than Norwood. One Dutchman who planned to visit Virginia learned that the region "was full of creeks and their branches . . . and it was difficult to get across them, as boats were not always to be obtained, and the people were not very obliging."[23] At mid-century the number of horses mentioned in the Northampton records rose, but despite a 1665 order from the colonial assembly directing local citizens to maintain roads forty feet wide, unencumbered by logs and stumps so "that all his Majesties subjects may have free and safe passage about their occasions," direct overland communication within the county was limited.[24] The problems connected with land travel even affected religious ceremony. The local vestry reluctantly voted, for example, to establish a new cemetery, "Haveing taken into consideration the remote liveing of the [members] of this parrish from the church."[25]

The importance of water-borne transport in the lives of all of Northampton's residents cannot be sufficiently emphasized. Almost all visiting that took place in mid-century Northampton depended upon the possession of a boat. Even persons of small estate owned canoes which, according to one local historian, were modeled after Indian vessels.[26] Whatever the inspiration for the design, canoes figured prominently in the county court records. A man who borrowed one without permission risked a heavy fine.[27] More affluent colonists contracted with Northampton's boatwrights for more substantial crafts than canoes. By the early 1640s Eastern Shore shipbuilders—one of the few groups in this community with a vocational specialty other than farming—were producing shallops. These were small, open sailing boats equipped with oars. They made excellent coasting vessels. Many measured more than twenty feet in length.[28]

Even if one owned a solidly built shallop, water travel required a combination of skill and luck. A short voyage along the Bay side could suddenly be transformed into a dangerous adventure. Captain Smith learned this when an unexpected "gust of wind, rayne, thunder, and lightening" drove his three-ton sailing barge in the opposite direction from that which he had charted.[29] Some years later a large ship named the *Phenix* was driven aground near Cherrystone Creek and lost all her "guns, Ammunition furniture Tackle and Apparrell with all goods wares and marchandizes."[30] Violent weather—or the fear of it—obviously reduced the colonists' opportunity to develop broad social networks. Throughout this period the environment hindered communication between friends and families, and the farther the distance traveled, the greater the possibility of mishap. We should remember these conditions when we turn our attention to the free blacks. While they spent most of their lives on isolated farms, they also risked the hazards of local travel in order to maintain strong ties with persons living in other parts of the county.

Northampton's physical isolation played a major role in shaping the character of its internal as well as its external politics. From the colony-wide perspective, the Bay created ambivalence; it highlighted differences. To be sure, people living on the Eastern Shore accepted the authority and legitimacy of the government at Jamestown. But at the same time, the very presence of the Chesapeake promoted a sense of independence. Even before Englishmen settled on the Eastern Shore, the Accomack Indians felt the pull of conflicting loyalties. On the one hand, they were tied by language and culture to the members of the Powhatan Confederacy that dominated the lower reaches of the James and York rivers. Despite these links, however, they valued their separation from their more aggressive western brethren. As Laughing King explained, "they on the West would invade them [the Accomacks], but . . . they want Boats to crosse the Bay."[31]

III

Interest in settling the Eastern Shore developed slowly among the English. As we have noted, Captain Smith explored the area, but his reports generated little enthusiasm for plantations across the Bay. In 1614 Sir Thomas Dale, a man remembered primarily as the author of a draconian code entitled *Lawes Divine, Morall and Martiall*, carved out a small settlement on the peninsula not far from Smith's Island. This venture was known appropriately enough as Dale's Gift. Within a few days, however, its promoters abandoned the Eastern Shore. The failure of Dale's Gift probably surprised no one.[32] During this period, maladministration on both sides of the Atlantic called the survival of the entire colony into question, and these problems exacerbated the difficulty of maintaining regular contact with people living on the eastern side of the Chespeake. Governor George Yeardley changed all this. It is from his administration that we date permanent English settlement on the Eastern Shore. Yeardley, appointed to office by the Virginia Company of London, arrived in the colony in 1618. His governorship coincided with the discovery of tobacco as a major export and with the establishment of the House of Burgesses. While Yeardley supposedly served the Company's interests, he also rarely missed an opportunity to advance his own prosperity. Men and women sent to the New World to produce profits for the Virginia Company often found themselves working for Yeardley or for one of his powerful friends.[33] The Governor saw the Eastern Shore as a particularly advantageous place to establish new plantations, and while he visited there on official business, everyone suspected that Yeardley was lining his own pockets.[34]

The Eastern Shore became a county in 1632, one of eight original Virginia shires. The history of county institutions on this side of the Bay was convoluted in the extreme and one cannot understand this complex story apart from the ambitions of the local gentry. Indeed, the shifting county lines between 1632 and 1673 provide an index to the political fortunes of certain dominant families. The Eastern Shore was initially named Accomack County, and the members of the county court, a group of local justices appointed by the governor, recorded their first meeting on January 7, 1633. A decade later the county was renamed Northampton. Possibly this change pleased Obedience Robins, a man born in Northampton, England, and who at mid-century happened to be the county's most powerful planter. Robins died in 1663, and almost immediately the Virginia government ordered the Eastern Shore divided into two separate counties, Northampton and Accomack.[35] Robins's principal rival, Colonel Edmund Scarborough, apparently engineered this decision in order to advance his own real estate schemes. As we shall learn, Scarborough's arrogance was boundless, and he collected a long list of enemies. It is not surprising, therefore, that when Scarborough died in 1670 the county was reunited into a single political unit called Northampton. This action was without precedent. The Virginia Assembly noted tartly that "Whereas the late disturbance in the Counties of Accomacke and Northampton can by noe better meanes bee composed or setled than by reduceing the Said Two Counties into one, Itt is ordered that both the Said Counties bee united and Soe remaine one County untill there shall appeare good cause againe to devide them."[36] While consolidation may have temporarily cooled tempers, it flew in the face of demographic reality. By the 1670s the population of the Eastern Shore had dispersed so broadly that it required two county courts to settle its disputes. In 1673 Accomack reappeared on the political map, this time for good.

The influence of the local grandees resulted in part from Northampton's physical separation from Jamestown. The big planters on the Eastern Shore forged commercial links with merchants in Holland, New England, and New Netherland, direct contacts with the outside world that did not depend upon persons living on the other side of the Bay.[37] The existence of this extensive trade network may have convinced some Northampton residents that they could survive quite well without Jamestown's interference. In 1652 a group of planters disgruntled about high colonial taxes and poor communications with the Virginia government described the "Countie of Northampton [as] disjoynted and sequestred from the rest of Virginia." The men who signed this petition were apparently attempting to take advantage of confusion created by the English Civil War. In any case, they called for "Annual Choyce of Magistrates" and local determination of "All Causes, Suite[s] or Tryalls (of what nature soever)" originating within the county.[38] Colony rulers put a quick end to such rebellious notions, but within a few years the House of Burgesses granted concessions to Northampton that were not given to other Virginia shires. In 1656, for example, the colonial legislature allowed the Northampton County court to draw up "customes" concerning local Indians and manufacturing so long as these practices did not clash with the laws of England and Virginia. And in 1658 the Burgesses ruled that because "of the greate distance between Northampton countie and James Cittie," no one could appeal a case beyond the county court unless the dispute involved 3200 lbs. of tobacco or £32 sterling, substantial sums in mid-century Virginia.[39]

Population figures are difficult to establish for any seventeenth-century Virginia county, and even though the Northampton records are fairly complete for this period, we still possess only a very rough estimate of the number of residents. One person who composed a piece modestly entitled A Perfect Description of Virginia in 1649 claimed that approximately fifteen thousand English people had settled in the colony. Of this number, "some English about a thousand are seated upon the Acamake-shore by Cape Charles, (where Captaine Yeardly is chief Commander) now called the County of Northampton."[40] It was a good guess. Recent calculations suggest that between 7 and 8 percent of the colony's tithables, persons whose names appeared on the tax lists, were resident on the East Shore. Despite problems of analysis created by alterations in the county's boundaries, it appears that the number of tithables increased slowly over the course of the century, rising from approximately 340 in 1644 to 707 in 1662.[41]

Rough population statistics, especially those documenting growth, provide a grossly misleading picture of what conditions were like in the Chesapeake colonies during the seventeenth century. Considering the unhealthiness of this environment, it is surprising that the population increased at all. In 1671 Governor William Berkeley observed in a somewhat astonishingly matter-of-fact fashion that "heretofore not one of five escaped the first year."[42] The major killers were contagious diseases, smallpox, malaria, dysentery, and while almost everyone has read grisly tales of death in Captain John Smith's Jamestown, few modern scholars realized until quite recently that the terrible rate of mortality continued almost to the end of the century. As late as 1679 persons contemplating visiting Virginia were warned that people die "by thousands sometimes of the epidemical disease of the country."[43] Such rumors had a basis in fact. Before 1680 the life expectancy in the Chesapeake colonies for a migrant was only about forty years. Seventy percent of the males who transferred from England to Maryland, for example, died before celebrating their fiftieth birthday. Approximately half of the children born in this region were dead before age twenty, a quarter before age one. A majority of the marriages recorded in seventeenth-century Maryland were broken within seven years by the death of one of the partners. Indeed, the threat of early death pervaded the Chesapeake, and no one—neither rich nor poor, black nor white—could escape the insecurity.[44]

IV

By the middle of the seventeenth century, Northampton had become a highly stratified society. Within this hierarchy, each group depended in some way upon other groups, although to paraphrase George Orwell, some were clearly more dependent than others. A man's place in the chain was determined in part by wealth and in part by race. Neither attribute at this time translated neatly into high or low social status. Of course, a rich Englishman stood a better chance of entering the county's ruling elite than did an Angolan slave, but to depict Northampton society solely in terms of class or race would be misleading. Some prosperous blacks, for example, found considerable room in which to maneuver. It is important, therefore, to describe the social order as a contemporary might have done. Certainly, people living on the Eastern Shore knew who the great planters were and easily distinguished them from lesser planters. These were things that men and women picked up in the course of their daily routine, and a modern historian who attempted to classify Northampton colonists solely on the basis of their standing on tax lists surely would miss the complexity of the county's social fabric.

It is possible to divide the population of seventeenth-century Northampton into seven separate groups. At the pinnacle of this structure, one would have discovered powerful persons who lived in England or in other parts of Virginia and who rarely, if ever, visited Northampton. Despite their absence, however, these people—royal governors, English administrators, and well-connected London merchants—affected county affairs, and even the most affluent Eastern Shore planters depended upon these men for favors. Within the county community the great planters domina ed public life. One report written in 1675 referred to these shire leaders as "the better sort of people"; perhaps the term "local gentry" would serve just as well.[45] Below them came a large, undifferentiated mass of free white planters. The next major group consisted of indentured servants, men and women serving a master for a stated number of years in exchange for passage to the New World. The county also contained slaves and Indians, and the seventh level, although by no means the lowest one on this scale, was the free blacks.[46] Through interaction with members of other groups, in court or in commerce, one discovered where one stood. There was nothing abstract about this ranking system. It had no meaning outside the face-to-face contacts that brought persons of different levels together. This loosely defined structure formed the social context in which men expressed values, worked out patterns of behavior suitable for various kinds of encounters, and developed private strategies for survival. One can appreciate the achievements and failures of a particular group only by understanding the full social environment in which they lived.

Everyone in Northampton recognized the importance that powerful outsiders could have upon their lives. The county was part of a large, complex network of contacts reaching out to London, Boston, New Amsterdam, and Jamestown. High-ranking men sometimes visited the Eastern Shore. Governors Yeardley and Bennett, for example, journeyed across the Bay, and during Bacon's Rebellion Governor Berkeley sought refuge there. When such gentlemen were present, they assumed control of the county's political institutions, and the local planters used these rare occasions to obtain special grants and privileges. For the most part, however, outsiders communicated with Eastern Shore settlers through orders written in Jamestown, contracts drafted in London, and commands sent from Whitehall. These links were irregular and unpredictable. When a member of the Northampton gentry dispatched a letter to the outside, he did not know if the addressee was still alive, or if alive, whether he remembered the peculiar circumstances of his Eastern Shore correspondent.

The great planters of Northampton resembled the lesser gentry of many western European nations. They were perhaps a bit poorer and less polished than were their counterparts in England and France, but they aspired to the same dominance over rural society. The gentry of Northampton was a small group, not more than a dozen families at any given time. For most of the century, the Robinses and Scarboroughs were the most prominent Eastern Shore leaders, but men with other surnames earned the right to be called great planters. Littletons, Stones, Burdetts, Yeardleys, Charltons, and Potts amassed considerable estates and gained a share of political power. Men from these families also sat on the county courts or served in the Virginia House of Burgesses. They married their sons and daughters to the children of other great planters.[47] Some Northampton gentry, no doubt, were of middle-class origins in England, aggressive merchant sons, men on the make, for as one writer in this period noted, Virginia was a fine place for "many Gentlemen [who] have unsettled themselves with a desire to better their fortunes in remote places."[48] However modest their genealogies may have been, these ambitious migrants assumed the right to rule and insisted upon receiving from their neighbors the same deference that might have been paid to a landed gentlemen in Kent or Suffolk. At mid-century the ranks of this group were still relatively open, and newcomers occasionally gained admission to the county court.[49]

Without a large estate a man, of course, could not claim to be a great planter. Indeed, in Northampton social status correlated closely with personal wealth. Local gentlemen usually built up their holdings through arduous work, hard bargaining, and sheer luck. A major factor in achieving economic success in this society was land, and some planters possessed a great deal of it. At one time Edmund Scarborough owned no less than one-quarter of Virginia's entire Eastern Shore.[50] His peers constantly sought new acreage on which to raise tobacco, corn, and livestock. The county court records are filled with these land transactions; some land came through headrights, other tracts through purchase. On January 11, 1641, for example, Obedience Robins demanded the court award him "two thousand acres of land for the transportation of 40 severall persons whose names are hereunder specified."[51]

Robin's grant was unusually large, but like him, other Northampton gentry routinely translated laborers into land. Because of the great size of these grants, the members of the gentry could engage in land speculation, something denied the smaller planters. In fact, for the county's economic elite land was a source of disposable income. It sold in Northampton for as much as a shilling an acre, a substantial sum.[52] The price must have placed land out of the reach of many people, for as the records reveal, it was not uncommon for men to rent or lease all the land that they cultivated.

In addition to land and tobacco, great planters served as merchants for smaller Northampton planters. Stephen Charlton rented out one of his boats for five pounds sterling. Other gentlemen owned mills or invested in light manufacturing, salt and shoes, for example, endeavors which freed them from total dependence upon tobacco.[53] Since the price for this staple was notoriously unpredictable it made good economic sense to diversify one's activities, and while Virginians were forever advocating diversification, the records show that the great planters of the Eastern Shore were actually in the best position to act upon this advice.[54]

The problem with this general description of the Northampton gentry is that it is altogether too benign. By confining our discussion to land and houses, to coasting vessels and tobacco crops—as many Virginia historians have done—we have given an incomplete picture of these men. The great planters of Scarborough's generation were hard-driving, grasping individuals. Mid-century Virginia society was too raw, too unsettled, to produce a person like William Byrd II. In 1726 that gentleman claimed that he lived "like one of the patriarchs, I have my flocks and my herds, my bond-men, and bond-women, and every soart of trade amongst my own servants, so that I live in a kind of independance of every one, but Providence."[55] For him, everything was under control. He could afford to be reflective about his condition.[56]

In 1650, however, a major planter would not have written in such a manner. The leaders of this period were fiercely independent people, competitive, materialistic, frequently truculent. Everything was most certainly not under control for them. They had their hands full merely surviving from year to year. No doubt, extreme privatism has been a defining characteristic of other societies. Such a set of values is often associated with frontier settlements, especially those which have promised instant wealth. One could find persons of this turn of mind in more established communities. As late as mid-century, Virginia had no generally accepted intellectual or religious system, such as Puritanism, to temper the planters' acquisitiveness. In time, customs and traditions would evolve in Virginia, elaborate rituals of authority that took place at the county court houses or on the racetracks, but in Scarborough's

Northampton the gentry were still unsure of themselves.[57] And, like the men who inhabited Captain Smith's Jamestown, they were quick to violence. As one historian has explained, "the men who governed Virginia in the 1640s, 1650s, and 1660s whether under king or Commonwealth, showed themselves to be only a little less ruthless than those who dominated the colony in the boom period [1620s]."[58]

Gentry values found untrammeled expression in the exploitation of dependent laborers. As in other plantation societies of the New World, land without workers produced little wealth. But with a large supply of servants and slaves to perform a score of tedious agricultural tasks, the great planters managed to wrest substantial profits from the soil. The unskilled fieldhands were primarily objects in a commercial process, like tools, seed, and hogsheads. In 1648 an Englishman wrote to a planter on the Eastern Shore that he had heard that Virginians regarded servants as "more advantageous . . . than any other *commodities*."[59] It did not much matter to the planters of this period who toiled for them. Whites, blacks, Indians, all comers were fair game in the scramble for wealth. Not for another quarter-century did the Virginia gentry worry a great deal about the race of their labor force.[60] Anthropologist Sidney Mintz has written extensively about the planters of the Caribbean, but his observations on this point are valid for the Chesapeake at mid-century; "the planters were, in one important respect, quite without prejudice: they were willing to employ any kind of labor, and under any institutional arrangements, as long as the labor force was politically defenseless enough for the work to be done cheaply and under discipline."[61] Some planters surely were less exploitive than were other gentlemen.[62] On the whole, however, the relation between masters and servants, between the great planters and the rest of the community, was crudely defined in terms of return on investment. It was against this background that dependent people devised strategies to survive in Northampton County.

Of all the great planters of the Eastern Shore, Edmund Scarborough II left the most complete record of his activities. In the 1620s Scarborough and his father emigrated to Virginia from Norfolk, England. They apparently came to the New World looking for fresh economic opportunities. Certainly the family possessed considerable resources. A brother who remained in England became a member of Parliament and personal physician to three kings. The senior Scarborough received appointment as one of the first Accomack (Northampton) justices of the peace, a sure sign of his wealth and influence. Edmund's father died in 1635, and for the next thirty-six years Colonel Edmund Scarborough dominated county affairs.[63]

Making money seems to have been the major passion in Scarborough's life. The range of his economic interests was extraordinary, and he exploited every new opportunity, be it legal or not, that promised to produce a few pounds sterling. Not only did Scarborough grow tobacco and speculate in land, he also tried his hand at the manufacture of salt and shoes. At one time he employed nine shoemakers in a factory on the Eastern Shore. He became a leading merchant and by midcentury the Colonel's ships carried local goods as far as New England and Florida. The center of commercial activities, however, appears to have been in New Netherland. During the 1650s, Scarborough purchased large numbers of slaves in New Amsterdam and transported them to Northampton where they brought him additional headrights. Sometimes his adventures ran afoul of the law. Despite his posture as a great Indian fighter, a defender of the Eastern Shore against the Indian peril, he sold arms and ammunition to the local tribes. This blatant breach of Virginia statute led to one of several arrest warrants issued against the Colonel.[64]

One was well advised not to cross Scarborough. In personal exchanges he obtained his way by one means or another, and in the county records he comes across not as an efficient entrepreneur, but as a wily brigand. His dealings with the Indians reveal the extent of his self-seeking. Over the years he developed an extensive trade with the local tribes, and common sense alone would seem to dictate that he should have maintained harmonious relations with his commercial partners. But in this case, common sense is an unreliable guide. For reasons that are not entirely clear, Scarborough became pathologically enraged when he thought the Indians had done him some wrong. In 1651 Scarborough and a party of locally recruited soldiers surprised some Indians at Occohannock Creek, where the Virginians "shot at and slashed [them] with their sabres and long hunting knives." Several Indians were dragged back in chains.[65] This unauthorized raid angered the other members of the Northampton court, the very people whom Scarborough claimed he had protected. They explained that the Colonel and his friends "did in a hostile manner contrary to the known laws of Virginia . . . raise a body of men, and marched among the Indians to take or kill the king of Pocomoke."[66] This personal vendetta had among other things endangered the lives and property of English settlers who had no controversy with the Indians.

By the late 1660s Scarborough was openly ignoring certain legal obligations. In one celebrated debt case he flaunted his position. A prominent London merchant, Daniel Fairfax, sued Scarborough for arrears amounting to almost a thousand pounds, and when the Virginian refused to pay, Fairfax enlisted the assistance of Lord Arlington, then Secretary of the Privy Council. Arlington instructed Governor Berkeley to collect the money, but as Berkeley soon discovered, Scarborough had powerful friends at court. Charles II personally ordered Berkeley to hold up the execution, since in the words of Berkeley, Scarborough had "more equity in his cause than I [Berkeley] could know of." This royal intervention amazed Berkeley; he was not about to call the King's judgment into question. The Governor himself was well represented at the Stuart court, but the Scarborough letter was "the first that ever I received from the Royal Highness of this nature."[67]

Scarborough's career raises troubling questions about the social structure of seventeenth-century Northampton. If other great planters behaved as Scarborough did, aggressively, even violently, advancing their own material interests at every turn, then what was everyday life like for the rest of the Eastern Shore population? Did dependent men and women survive by truckling to the whims of powerful gentry? Was the dominance of the great planters complete? To provide simple answers to these questions is impossible. However, the example of Scarborough does point to the critical role of gentry factionalism, as it affected all ranks of society.

In the period before Bacon's Rebellion, this factionalism prevented the gentry from achieving unchallenged hegemony over the small and middling planters. Had the great planters of the Eastern Shore stood together as did the major slave-holders of the nineteenth-century South, they might have exercised almost unlimited control over Northampton society. However, this they did not do. Throughout the period of our study vitriolic feuds divided the gentry. Obedience Robins and Edmund Scarborough openly despised one another.[68] In perhaps the most telling evidence of Robins's ability to check Scarborough's expansionism, his death was immediately followed by the implementation of Scarborough's long-sought scheme to divide the Eastern Shore into two separate counties. Colonel Scarborough's survey of the region not surprisingly awarded most of the land on the Eastern Shore to his own shire of

Accomack.[69] A decade later, the Northampton gentry were still grumbling about Scarborough's treachery. In 1676 a group of leading planters told crown commissioners sent to investigate the causes of Bacon's Rebellion that "*Whereas* our county some yeares since was contrary to our expectation divided into two Counties to our great Detriment and Loss notwithstanding the great advantage Coll. *Scarborough*, then made and procured to the County of *Acomock* against Lieut. Coll. *Waters* then his fellow Burgess." The ineffectual William Waters, the Northampton Survey Commissioner, had proved to be no match for Scarborough. The Northampton gentry contended that it was "Reasonable that our County may be . . . Inlarged as theirs [his]." The document was signed by Argoll Yeardley, William Spencer, John Custis, Junior, and seven other major planters.[70]

Divisions within the gentry may help us to explain how certain seemingly marginal persons flourished on the Eastern Shore. Political factionalism created social cleavages—economic and political niches—that ambitious men could exploit for their own benefit. If a patron failed, one might turn to a rival. It was a dangerous game, but as we have seen, people like Anthony Johnson were extremely sensitive to shifting power relationships within the county community, and in part, they owed their success to disputes between the great planters of Northampton.

The majority of the population of the Eastern Shore at mid-century was comprised of small planters. Unlike the great planters the members of this group left frustratingly little record of their activities. Their names appeared regularly on the tithable lists, testimony to the fact that however obscure their lives may have been, they did not escape the tax collector. In terms of personal wealth, of course, "small planter" is a broad classification, and persons within this group ranged from the destitute to the moderately well-to-do. Inventories drawn up in the 1640s provide a rough indication of the small planters' standard of living. One, John Pope, died in June 1642, leaving his wife and daughter an estate valued at only 139 pounds of tobacco. The inventory is a grim document, especially when we consider that men like Pope came to the New World in search of quick economic returns.

	pounds tobacco
Item one old Gowne	040
One Kettle pott and pott hokes	020
one old Ketle	010

	pounds tobacco
one old Chest att	010
one old Weedeing hoe	005
one old hilling hoe	003
one Tray	004
3 old Splitt boules att	003
2 old Axes att	005
1 old Case att	001
1 shott bagg and horne	003
one matt att	005
1 Cropp of tobacco att	030
The hoggs all dead. Summa totalis	139[71]

We can assume that Pope arrived in Virginia as an indentured servant. He managed to accumulate the crude tools necessary for tobacco cultivation and little else. Judging by the number of times that the appraisers used the word "old," one suspects that even the figure 139 may have been generous. These meager belongings did nothing to lessen the family's poverty, for as the Northampton court discovered, "John Pope deceased doth stand ingaged unto George Wright the Summe of three pounds tenn shillings sterling and the quantity of Three hundred pounds of tobacco." The court advised Wright to obtain satisfaction "wheresoever it shall bee found etc."[72]

In contrast to John Pope, Edward Bestwick was not impoverished. As a small planter, he attained a modest level of material well-being. The court records reveal that during the 1630s, Bestwick sued people and was sued in return for substantial amounts of tobacco. In 1635 the local justices ordered a man to pay Bestwick the remaining 72 lbs. of a 600-lb. debt. On another occasion, he and a neighbor lost a case involving 300 pounds of tobacco.[73] By the standards of the great planters, these were not excessive sums, but there is no question that Bestwick held his own in this society. When he died, court-appointed appraisers inventoried his estate. While his possessions were valued at only 100 pounds of tobacco, Bestwick clearly lived better than did his neighbor, John Pope.

The following list contains several items that Pope did not own, a sow, a house, poultry, a gun, but even with these possessions, Bestwick's life on the Eastern Shore must have been haunted by uncertainty. The lack of clear title to his "plantation" meant that however well he cultivated his fields, his economic situation remained insecure.

Edward Bestwick his Inventory

An Inventory of all the goodes and Estate that Edward Bestwick dyed possessed of, and praized according to Order of Court by Thomas Powell and James Bruce the 8th day of June 1641.

Imprimis one old bed Rugg an old boulster
    Item an Iron Kettle, and old Iron pott and pott hookes
    Item one old Pale
    Item 3 old Indian bowles
    Item 2 Indian Trays
    Item 2 sifters
    Item a Ladle
    Item an Iron hooke to hang a pott on
    Item a small fowleing piece unfixed
    Item an old sword
    Item one good Felling axe and another broken one
    Item a hatchett and a hand sawe
    Item two hammers
    Item 3 earthen pottes
    Item one Chest, and Case and an old boxe with a broken Leede [lid]
    Item an old skillett, 3 old spoones and a porrenger
    Item 2 old Mattes
    Item a shott bagg and powder horne
    Item 3 henns and a Cock
    Item one sowe and a smoothing Iron
    Item an Iron pestle
    Item the Plantation being in question having noe Lease about Eight Acres Cleered and a Dwelling howse

All the above mentioned particulars being valued at 100 pounds tobacco as appeareth by the oathes of James Bruse and Thomas Powell. . . .

Debtes that was oeing, and due to Edward Bestwick Item from Capt. Hawley, 2 poundes powder.
    John Towlson two poundes powder . . . . .
    Robert West old debt . . . . 035 pounds tobacco
    Mr. Major old debt 060
    James Davis two Indian bowles . . . .
Item from Mr. Berryman two Virginia hhdes. halfe a pounde of black thred and a Munworth Capp
Item John Cuttes one Indian bowle.[74]

Unlike members of the local gentry, the small planters were seldom surrounded by gangs of dependent laborers. Their homes were large enough to shelter only a few adults. No dwellings from this period have survived on the Eastern Shore, but we know from the court records that in 1645 Richard Buckland, a small planter, complained that he had paid 240 pounds of tobacco and "an Ewe Kidd" to Mathew Pett for building a house "Twenty Foote long with a welch Chimney . . . and Fifteene Foote Broade with a partition and buttery in it." Unfortunately, Pett died before completing the task.[75] It would have been difficult for a Pope or Bestwick to purchase such a home. In all probability, Bestwick's "Dwelling howse" was a one-room shack, just enough to protect him and his wife from the weather. A few planters in this group owned a servant or two, but for the most part, they lived in small units. Of the 150 households listed in 1664 by the Northampton County clerk, 103 consisted of fewer than four persons.[76] Sometimes these households were composed of a man, his wife, and their dependent children. Others were made up of several single men, individuals who probably had completed terms as indentured servants but who lacked the financial means either to establish a family or to purchase servants of their own. Again, the contrast with the great planters is significant. Persons like Scarborough arrived in Virginia as freemen; they brought money and connections with them. But the overwhelming majority of small planters came to the Chesapeake colonies as indentured servants, and simply by avoiding death managed to reach the ranks of Northampton's free planters.[77]

We must not exaggerate the cohesiveness of the small planters. However many attributes they shared as Englishmen, migrants, and farmers, they were not conscious of forming a distinct social or economic class within the county community. Knowledge of this fact is crucial to understanding the character of Northampton's social structure at mid-century. The small planters were widely dispersed and they seldom came into contact with families living beyond the waters of a particular cove or inlet, and no county-wide institutions promoted a sense of common purpose with other small planters.[78] The contrast between these people and the members of the local elite is instructive. The great planters did in fact achieve self-awareness, if not cohesion, as a group. They perceived, even when they were battling for political dominance, the existence of common economic and social interests. They shared in the performance of local rituals of authority. Indeed, their bonds were regularly reinforced at meetings of the Northampton County court or at other official activities. The small planters obviously could not develop a comparable level of group consciousness. They were linked not to their peers but to a world market through the mediation of wealthy neighbors or distant merchants.[79]

The small planter's life revolved around his family, his house, and the next harvest—all equally fragile elements within this environment. From time to time, he and his neighbors gathered to trade stories and share a strong drink. If the planter was fortunate, he lived near one of Northampton's ordinaries, where "Beere Ale Wynes" were dispensed.[80] On one Sunday at least, more than twenty people in Accomack who should have been attending church were caught swilling at the home of John Cole, a licensed tavern keeper.[81] But for most of the inhabitants of the Eastern Shore such events must have been rare. The people who migrated to Virginia during this period left behind in England a rich heritage of folk customs, local holidays and market days, special times for games and fairs. The traditional Maytime games in Kent, for example, were greeted in the 1660s with "a kind of rural triumph, expressed by the country swains in a morris-dance, with the old music of tabor and pipe . . . with all agility and cheerfulness imaginable."[82] The English agrarian calendar of the seventeenth century set aside times for work and for pleasure, and as often as not, customary pleasures blended in with the performance of farm work. According to Joan Thirsk, "Unlike the leisure pastimes of today, the recreations of Tudor and Stuart labourers were not merely a means of escape: they formed a kind of inherited art or ritual, centring round their daily occupations, and based upon the ordinary sights and sounds of the village."[83] By comparison, the Virginia calendar seemed dull, uneventful. The records contain no mention of games or songs or feasts.[84] There were no market days; towns did not exist. The year turned on making tobacco, a plant which even Virginians contemptuously called a "stinking weed." In this world, drinking at the ordinaries may well have served as an escape from the lonely drudgery of field labor.[85]

Living in a society dominated by avaricious gentry, and without strong communal bonds or any unifying ideology, the small planters tended to regard each other with marked suspicion. This lack of trust should come as no surprise. Men and women seldom arrived in Virginia within a family group. They were young and single, and during periods of illness and personal need, they had no kinfolk on whom they could depend.[86] Migration tore people from a web of human relationships that had provided a sense of secure social identity in England. On the Eastern Shore almost everyone was initially a stranger, a person stripped of public genealogy.[87] Many newcomers died in this anonymous state. But they were replaced each year by fresh waves of strangers, solitary individuals aggressively searching for the main chance in the New World.

As a group, the small planters never challenged the authority of the local gentry. There were several obvious explanations for this behavior. First, the small planters of the Eastern Shore accepted—along with most everyone else in the English-speaking world—the view that human society was a hierarchical structure, and while none of them expressed the idea quite so bluntly as did the seventeenth-century New England minister William Hubbard, they certainly agreed with him that, "It is not then the result of time or chance, that some are mounted on horse-back, while others are left to travell on foot. That some have with the Centurion, power to command, while others are required to obey."[88] And second, the small planter's sphere of daily activities—be they religious or political—was narrowly circumscribed by the peculiarities of local geography. His personal networks seldom extended beyond the world of his immediate neighbors. This limited scale of social organization coupled with a low level of literacy meant that the small planters did not develop a consciousness of having political and economic interests separate from those of the Scarboroughs and Robinses.[89] The gentry expected and usually received deference from the small planters, and since these gentlemen monopolized positions of authority and knowledge of legal procedures, they did not find it too difficult to maintain dominance over the rest of the county community.[90]

But it was one thing to consider the small planters as a group, quite another to deal with them as individuals. At any given time such a person, truculent, highly independent, schooled in a tradition of English rights, might not accept the part for which society had cast him. Thomas Parks and George Vaux were men of this stripe. Vaux apparently forgot how dangerous it was to speak ill of a gentleman. In 1643 he appeared in open court to beg the forgiveness of Captain Francis Yeardley, one of the most powerful settlers on the Eastern Shore. Vaux, it seems, "disparraged and defam'd Capt. Frauncis Yeardley and . . . Lay'd a most grose Aspersion upon the Reputation of the said Capt. Yeardley That the said Capt. Yeardley was on the bedd with Alice the wife of George Travellor with his hands under the Coates of the said Alice."[91] Apparently gentry did not behave in this manner, or if they did, the likes of George Vaux kept their mouths shut.

Thomas Parks committed an even more serious breach of social etiquette. According to several witnesses who gave depositions before the open court in 1643, Parks had defamed the good name of Argoll Yeardley, son of a former governor of Virginia and a person described in the court records as "Esquire Comaunder etc." Parks allegedly told a group of people sitting around Nathaniel Littleton's kitchen that despite what they might have heard, Yeardley's father was no gentleman, at least he had not been one in England. In fact, he had worked only as a tailor in a "Stall in Burchin Lane in London." And as for Argoll's mother, she "was a middwife not to the honourable cittizens but to bye blows." One horrified listener protested that Mrs. Yeardley had been "an honourable gentlewoman." Parks agreed, but insisted that this well-respected woman was the Governor's second wife and not the present Commander's mother. Moreover, as Parks reflected upon his various legal problems, he concluded he would never receive a fair hearing before the present members of the Northampton court, and so rather than trust to the integrity of the local gentry, he preferred to "goe to the Susquesehanocks and see what I can doe there."[92] This was too much. Not only had Parks called Argoll's pedigree into question—really the legitimacy of his claim to a place on the county court—but he also found the Indians more worthy of respect than was the assembled squirearchy. Not surprisingly, Commander Argoll Yeardley, Captain William Roper, Mr. William Andrewes, Mr. Edward Douglas, and Mr. Edmund Scarborough punished Parks for his contempt of authority with thirty lashes "upon his bare shoulders."[93]

Sometimes contempt turned to violence. If a court order struck a small planter as unwarranted or annoying, he might simply ignore it until he felt like dealing with the matter. The sheriff or other local authorities charged with law enforcement were well advised to leave these feisty individuals alone, but confrontations were inevitable. One September day in 1641 Andrew Jacob and two other men went to Thomas Wyatt's house to present "a Warrant directed from the Commander." When the three visitors arrived, Wyatt, his wife, and a laborer were busy hanging tobacco for curing. This was a difficult task for any planter, one not easily interrupted. No sooner had Jacob read the document than Wyatt's wife began insulting him, "and fell upon his face sayeing have you brought a Warrant for my husband you base

Rouge." The assault caught Jacob off guard. He did state, however, that if Mrs. Wyatt were not holding an infant in her arms, he would gladly give her "a Kick on the britch." She accepted the challenge, put down the child, and again began hitting Jacob over the head. What happened next is not entirely clear. Jacob claimed he pushed her away without laying a hand on her body. But this was not what John Broome, the laborer, saw. Up until this point he had been sitting on a joist hanging tobacco, and after the shoving, he cried, "Rougue do you strike a Weoman." Broome leapt to the floor, picked up a stanchion, and started beating poor Jacob upon the head. Thomas Wyatt now joined the attack. Jacob's friends, described as "weake and sickley," managed to separate the brawlers, but no sooner had they done so than Broome renewed the fight. The three visitors wisely decided to retreat. The Northampton court later fined Wyatt and Broome for battery.[94] By this time, of course, they had completed the harvest, and presumably Jacob had learned something about the limits of the Commander's authority over the common folk.

Most of the small planters came to Virginia as servants. It has been estimated that 75 percent of the white population were dependent laborers when they arrived in the New World.[95] As one reads the Northampton court records, one senses that these largely anonymous men and women—like the slaves of a later period of Southern history—powerfully shaped the character of daily life. They performed a variety of mundane tasks, grew tobacco, talked with their masters, gave depositions before the county justices when asked to do so; they were omnipresent.[96] And yet, however much they blended into the general social environment, they created uneasiness and distrust. The planters knew, perhaps from personal experience, that even the most contented laborer counted the days until freedom. The planter expected a good return on his investment. For him, the servant was simply a form of property. But the indentured workers refused to become "commodities." Throughout these decades they insisted upon being treated as human beings, and therein, of course, lay a constant source of social tension.

The recruitment of Chesapeake servants took place in England. It was there that men and women decided to try their luck on the Tobacco Coast. Other possibilities were available, for a young person from the countryside could just as easily have moved to London, Holland, or a New World colony other than Virginia.[97] Propagandists played a major role in persuading uncertain persons of the advantages of Virginia. Indeed, some writers depicted the colony as a land of milk and honey. Boys were hustled off to America "by flattering and great promises."[98] Servants learned that Virginia was "a place where food shall drop into their mouths."[99] One Englishman obviously familiar with the recruitment process explained that servants on the eve of departure talked only "of the pleasantness of the soyl of that Continent we were designed for . . . the temperature of the Air, the pleanty of Fowl and Fish of all sorts; the little labour that is performed or expected having so little trouble in it, that it rather may be accounted a pastime than anything of punishment."[100] Some servants assumed that they would receive free land at the conclusion of their contracts. Rumors and half-truths fed dreams, built up a level of expectation that the colony could not possibly fulfill. Thus, while it is true that most servants freely elected to transfer to the New World, they often did so on the basis of erroneous or incomplete information.[101] Certainly, the actual demands of plantation life shocked these recruits, and William Bullock, a pamphleteer writing in 1649, wisely counseled planters against men and women who "not finding what was promised, their courage abates, & their minds being dejected, their work is according."[102]

Servitude involved a formal, legally enforceable agreement. The terms of the covenant seemed simple enough. The servant provided physical labor for a period of years in exchange for the cost of transportation to the New World and maintenance during the time of service. In point of fact, however, these bargains often generated misunderstanding, and both master and servant were well advised to take great care in negotiations over specific details. Well-informed men and women signed indentures in England, spelling out quite clearly how long and under what conditions they would serve a Chesapeake planter. John Hammond, author of a pamphlet that described life on the Tobacco Coast, warned prospective servants ". . . to be sure to have your contract in writing and under hand and seal, for if you go over upon promise made to do this or that, or to be free or your own man, it signifies nothing." Hammond was a planter himself and knew from experience that only an "Indenture is . . . binding and observing."[103] For a variety of reasons, illiteracy, youth, naïveté, many men and women ignored Hammond's counsel. They took their chances, sailing to Virginia or Maryland in hopes of working out a suitable agreement with a local master. It was a major gamble. If they found no likely employer, the captain of the ship would sell them to anyone he pleased. The terms of these covenants, based upon the "custom of the country," depended upon an individual's age, and while the House of Burgesses constantly tinkered with the laws governing these servants, it generally expected them to labor from four to five years, or if the person was very young, until he or she reached the age of twenty-four.[104] According to statute, a Virginia master was enjoined to "provide for his servants competent dyett, clothing and lodging, and . . . he shall not exceed the bounds of moderation in correcting them beyond the meritt of their offences."[105] At the end of the contract period, servants "by custom" received three barrels of "Corne and Cloathes," enough goods presumably to give them an independent start.[106] What they did not obtain, however, was land, since the headright went not to the servant, but to the man who paid for the servant's transportation to America.

Sometimes freemen living in Northampton consented to become servants, usually for short periods of time and under conditions carefully defined by contract. These agreements often appeared in the records of the county court, and this evidence indicates that these particular laborers were older and better informed about the demands of life in Virginia than were servants who had just arrived. In fact, this group presumably consisted of individuals who had already completed an indenture but who found that they did not possess sufficient financial resources to establish a small plantation of their own. John Booth seems to have been such a person. This man's background is obscure. Edmund Scarborough petitioned the court for a headright of fifty acres in Booth's name, but from the available sources, it is impossible to tell when Booth actually took up residence on the Eastern Shore.[107] Whatever his personal history may have been, on November 1, 1640, he entered into a covenant with Captain William Roper, a justice on the county court. The terms of the agreement offered Booth an opportunity to become a small planter, equipped with tobacco plants, corn, and a breeding cow. By escaping taxes for a year, he may have even protected a small amount of savings.[108]

In sheer number, the men and women who arrived in Northampton as servants played a more significant role in determining the character of the society than did short-term laborers like Booth. Colonial historians no longer believe that England sent only thieves and rogues, whores and villains to the Chesapeake, at least it did not do so in the mid-seventeenth century.[109] Servants were drawn from all groups within the mother country, common laborers, skilled artisans, husband-

men, yeomen, even an occasional gentleman.[110] But whatever their
social origins—and the evidence bearing on this subject is quite thin—it
is certain that males far outnumbered females within the servant population, probably by a ratio as high as three to one. Moreover, the overwhelming majority of servants who landed in Virginia and Maryland
were young, generally ranging in age from seventeen to twenty-eight.
The group included a sizable contingent of boys and adolescents who
had not yet learned a skill or trade. And finally, servants traveled to this
part of America as solitary individuals. The decisions to move cut them
off from parents, and because of their youth and dependent status they
had had no opportunity in England to form families of their own.[111]

Those men and women who survived to the end of their contracts
may well have enjoyed modest status mobility relative to people who
remained in England, but at what price? The experience they had as
servants on the Eastern Shore affected their attitudes as freemen, and if
they endured five to seven years of abuse and degradation as adolescents, one might reasonably surmise at the very least that these unpleasant memories were not easily forgotten, and at the most that they
helped determine exploitative patterns of adult behavior. The indentured servants of the seventeenth century were not slaves, but for a significant portion of their lives they were property, men and women who
could be bought, sold, and passed on to the planter's heirs. And while
much has been made of the slave codes which governed colonial blacks,
almost no one has systematically considered the severe legal restraints
placed upon servants during a formative period of their lives. An institution that touched so many persons should be carefully examined before
we conclude that it was a blessing in disguise or that it was not "an appropriate introduction to the history of the slave trade."[112]

Virginia law allowed mistreated servants to petition to a county
court for relief, and they thereby gained what seemed a measure of legal
protection from cruel masters. A statute passed in 1642 gave servants
with "just cause of complaint" an opportunity to appeal directly to a
local justice. The law sounded equitable. But in all probability, it
required exceptional courage for a servant to take a master to court,
especially if that person had in fact behaved in a "harsh or unchristian-
like" manner, for the county commissioners usually only admonished
bad masters to mend their ways. The servant who complained still had
to live under the man's authority. In 1658, however, the colonial assembly rewrote the law governing servant petitions, insisting that only

after the servant had presented *prior* "notice to his master" could the servant protest to local officials about "bad usage." The Burgesses re-passed the act in 1662, entitling it "Against Runaway Servants," and it appears from the wording of the statute that the members of the legislature were more concerned about controlling unruly servants than about improving the quality of servant life.[113] Even under these constraints, a few servants petitioned for redress, but such actions were generally a waste of time. In Northampton County the great majority of servant complaints were decided in favor of the masters.[114]

Under these circumstances servants on the Eastern Shore often endured bad usage, a few out of fear of the master, others out of ignorance of the law. In 1640 a servant woman petitioned the Northampton court, begging protection from her former mistress, Mrs. John Wilkins. The case involved several bizarre, though significant, elements. The servant Elinor Rowe had apparently not recorded the slightest complaint against her mistress as long as she worked directly under Wilkins's supervision. But Rowe escaped. For reasons never fully explained in the records, Wilkins decided to swap her serving maid for that of Mrs. James Berry. Everyone considered the transfer permanent. When Wilkins began to express second thoughts, however, Elinor Rowe panicked. She informed the county court of Mrs. Wilkins's "unchristian like and violent oppression" and "her continuall strikeinge [,] Beateinge and abusing her [Rowe] with careless resolute Blowes." Rowe insisted that these attacks, for which there were witnesses, endangered her life, and she predicted that if the court ordered her to return to the Wilkins plantation, "shee shall doubtles be murthered." Rowe was fortunate. The justices allowed her to remain in the Berry Household to "serve her whole Indented tyme." The other maid probably bore the brunt of Wilkins's anger; no one seemed concerned about her welfare. The entire case, of course, revealed the weakness of the servant's legal position. Had Rowe not been sent to the Berrys, had she not understood her rights before the law, and had she not thrown herself on the mercy of the court, she might have been summarily shipped back to Mrs. Wilkins, and no one would have known of Rowe's suffering.[115]

Thomas Wood was not so lucky. This servant's suspicious death in the summer of 1640 forced the county court to convene a jury of inquest. Witnesses who came before this body testified that the boy led an unhappy life on the Walker plantation. Indeed, just before he died, Wood ran away from his master's farm and was found hiding in a

neighbor's "Calfe howse." This was not the boy's first attempt to escape
from Peter Walker, an individual whom even Edmund Scarborough
called "a cruell man." When Wood returned home, Walker ordered a
hired man, Samuel Lucas, to whip the servant. After he had done so,
Walker took a turn beating the boy with "a little twigge." There were
also stories that Lucas occasionally struck Wood with a rope "about the
bignes of a Finger." Others described the implement simply as "a little
Cord." All witnesses agreed, however, that the punishment had not
been particularly harsh or unusual; for according to one man, "a child
of tenne yeares ould might be soe whipped and receave noe hurtt tou-
chinge Life." Another person believed that a seven-year-old should have
been able to endure such blows. But, regardless of the way adults normally treated servant children on the Eastern Shore, the fact remained
that Wood died. Walker and his friends claimed that sickness killed the
servant, and the jury accepted this account, noting in its final report
that Wood's corpse looked no different than "anie man might be
dyeinge of the Scurvey beinge much swelled." [116] Whatever the cause
of Wood's death, the boy unquestionably had been abused, but because
he could not petition the county court he received no protection under
the law.

As one might expect, female servants—like female slaves in a later
period of Virginia history—were vulnerable to sexual exploitation by
their masters. The colonial assembly admitted that "dissolute masters"
sometimes fathered illegitimate children with servant women. The
major problem confronting the legislators was how to control such behavior. After all, the servant woman, whether pregnant or not, was still
a valuable article of property. And the logic of this dependent labor system dictated that "if a woman gott with child by her master should be
freed from that service it might probably induce such loose persons to
lay all their bastards to their masters." The Burgesses concluded, therefore, that immoral servant women should be compelled to serve out
their full indentures and at the end of their contracts be sold by
churchwardens for an additional two years. [117] The profits from this extended service went to the local vestry. Presumably, the mere threat of
this severe penalty helped servant girls summon up the courage to resist
their owners' advances. The masters, dissolute though they may have
been, gained the woman's full period of service and escaped punishment—a procedure not designed to promote self-restraint among the
masters.

Certainly, masters rarely took the loyalty of servants for granted. Owners believed that unless they exercised constant vigilance, dependent workers would defy authority by running away, by stealing goods, or by slipping away to "unlawful meetings." [118] There seemed no limit to potential servant mischief. The members of the House of Burgesses, especially after 1660, described the danger from indentured servants in shrill, even hysterical rhetoric. In 1668, for example, they declared in the preamble to a law dealing with runaways that previous attempts to thwart escapes had failed "through the wickednesse of servants who at and before their arrivall plott and contrive how they may free themselves from their master, by running to neighboring plantations." The average planter found himself at a considerable disadvantage. He was helpless to chase after the culprits, for he had "not servants enough left (whome he can trust) to follow and pursue those runawayes." [119] Masters watched for suspicious movements; they worried that other planters would steal their servants. According to Virginia statute, dependent workers were forbidden to leave a plantation without a "lycence." [120] Any planter could demand that a stranger produce this pass, and in that way, it was thought that outnumbered masters could maintain control over a growing labor force. The Burgesses assured obedient servants that they need not fear these restraints, for "if they keep within the bounds of their duty, [they] are in noe way damnified by the severity of this act, and it is hoped they will be soe when *they know soe many spies are upon them.*" [121]

Despite the presence of "many spies," Northampton servants often managed to slip away. As we have already seen, Thomas Wood ran from his master whenever he had an opportunity, but either because of youth or inexperience, he never made good his escape. Other servants apparently took time off with no intention of permanently leaving their master's service. Perhaps they wanted to visit friends or needed a break from the tedious agricultural routine. Whatever their purpose, the members of the county court dealt with these offenders in a curious manner. They simultaneously upheld the awful sovereignty of Virginia law while demonstrating their own capacity for mercy, a judicial strategy that may have frightened first offenders into obedience. After hearing evidence, the court would hand down a harsh punishment, ten to twenty lashes, but before the sentence could be carried out, the local justices pardoned the defendant. A second violation, of course, would bring the whip, but for the present the thankful servant was free on his own good behavior.[122] In 1642, for example, George Traveller hauled his servant Joan before the court, claiming that she "hath absented herselfe out of her said Masters and Mistress service without License of her said Master or Mistresse." The Northampton justices decided that Joan's actions merited "Tenn Lashes upon her bare shoulders." But the next entry in the county records revealed that the judicial process was intended largely as a threat, a carefully staged means to impress upon Joan the seriousness of her offense. "Upon the petition of George Traveller," the clerk noted, "the punishment ordered to be inflicted upon Joane servaunt unto the said Traveller is hereby remitted."[123] A few months later John Wilkins urged the court to chastise his servant, John Williams, for absenting himself "from his Masters service." On this occasion Argoll Yeardley persuaded Wilkins to show compassion. After this public courtroom exchange, no doubt performed for Williams's benefit, the court ordered, "That for the next offence in the like nature [which] shalbe comitted by the said Williams the said John Williams shall have Twenty lashes upon his bare shoulders as a punishment."[124]

Sometimes groups of Northampton servants conspired to escape. In 1638 several servants decided that conditions on the Eastern Shore had become unbearable, and they hatched a plot to run away to New Netherland. The details of this case reveal how thoroughly some dependent laborers hated being servants, and more, to what lengths they were willing to go to obtain freedom. John Neale assumed leadership. Whenever he had a chance to speak with other servants, usually when their masters sent them to purchase fish from "Robert the Ferryman," Neale would explain his plans. He informed one servant that "hee [Neale] had forty yardes of cloath to make every one a suyte that wente with him." Moreover, he guaranteed his co-conspirators good jobs in "the dutch plantation," and lest anyone doubt his veracity, Neale pointed out that he spoke "very good dutch."[125]

One servant, William Abraham, found these plans enticing, but he recognized that the trip from Northampton to New Amsterdam was long and dangerous. One day while he was working in the fields brooding about the logistical problems, his master's son, John Powell, happened to mention that he owned "a booke to learne to speake the Indyan tongue." Abraham jumped at the opportunity, immediately offering the boy several pipes in exchange for the book. With knowledge of the local Indian language, a group of servants might safely make their way northward. And perhaps in his excitement, Abraham said more than he ought to to young Powell. He asked rhetorically, "wherefore should wee stay here and bee slaves . . . [when we] may goe to another place and live like gentlemen." Powell wondered if Abraham intended to journey to the "Dutch Plantation," pointing out in passing that those servants who had tried that route before ended up being "kno[cked] in the head," presumably by the Indians. Abraham dismissed these stories. They were spread by the masters to discourage servants from running away. The plot failed in the end. Apparently, Powell told his father what the servants were planning, and a decade later Abraham was still toiling on the Eastern Shore.[126]

Most servants of the Eastern Shore, of course, remain anonymous. We know about people like John Neale, Thomas Wood, and Elinor Rowe because they did something unusual that brought them to the attention of the members of the Northampton court. The great majority of the county's dependent workers probably chose to bide their time, accepting personal discomfort and sexual privation, believing all the while that they would become planters, even the possessors of servants like themselves. Still, one cannot help concluding that the experience of being reduced to a commodity, to chattel, left scars on those men and women who lived long enough to move up into the ranks of the county's free planters. This point should be stressed. The small planters of Northampton were persons who learned about proper forms of behavior, about acceptable patterns of human relations, about exploitation and competition, about "careless resolute Blowes" and embittering frustrations, while they were servants. The culture of these people was not an English culture neatly transferred to America and sustained there through a period of dependence and vulnerability. Rather, their culture was a peculiar hybrid, part English, part Virginian, the unique creation of indentured servitude and a raw plantation economy. One would not expect that young people schooled in this environment developed a deep sense of compassion for other men and women. They learned as adolescents to survive as best they could. In the process, they were transformed into aggressive, competitive, highly individualistic Virginians.

4

The Free Blacks of the Eastern Shore

Within this inchoate social system, some blacks gained freedom. Their names regularly appeared in official Northampton documents of the mid-seventeenth century, not as anonymous tithables or as common lawbreakers, but as assertive men and women who acquired property, formed families, and provided for their children's welfare. Indeed, the richness of the surviving records makes it possible to reconstruct in surprising detail the lives of these particular black planters. What one discovers from these sources is that while these were people of exceptional ability, they did not flourish by separating themselves from the rest of the county community. Rather, they became part of a complex human network, and it was their success in dealing with white planters, great and small, servants and slaves, that in large measure explains their viability on the Eastern Shore.

The size of Northampton's black population can be established with a fair degree of certainty for the years after 1660. The tithable list for 1664 reveals that sixty-two blacks lived in the county, representing about 14 percent of the total number of tithables. By 1677 these figures had risen only slightly, seventy-five blacks making up 16 percent of the Northampton tithables. Edmund S. Morgan, who analyzed these records with great care, found 1,043 names on all the surviving lists between 1664 and 1677 (four years were lost) of which 101 were black men and women. Of much greater interest for the present investigation is the number of free blacks, persons clearly identified as independent householders on the tithable lists. The figure is larger than one would anticipate. Thirteen blacks, ten men and three women, were or became householders between 1664 and 1677. This seems a rather meager accomplishment until one realizes that 19 percent (ten out of fifty-three) of the black males in Northampton became householders. These are, of course, composite figures for the thirteen-year span.[1] The 1668 tithable list taken alone yields even higher percentages. In that year the sheriff discovered that approximately 29 percent of the Northampton blacks had gained freedom, a number that understandably impresses historians who have studied American race relations in later periods.[2] George M. Fredrickson, for example, noted, "Although we cannot determine with any accuracy how many free blacks there were in Virginia in the late seventeenth century, it would appear that they comprised a larger portion of the total black population than they would at any subsequent time during the slave era."[3]

The free blacks of the Eastern Shore possessed both family and given names. This fact is of great significance, for the presence of black family names in the Northampton records allows us to place individuals within specific kinship networks. Some names that appeared during this period were Sebastian Cane, Bashaw Ferdinando, John Francisco, Susan (Susanna) Grace, William Harman, Philip Mongum, Francis Payne (Pane or Paine), Emanuel (Manuel) Driggus (Rodriggus), Thomas Driggus, Mary Rodriggus, Tony King, Sara King, Tony Longo, Anthony Johnson, Mary Johnson, John Johnson, Richard Johnson, and Jane Gossall. This list is not exhaustive. Other free blacks—wives, daughters, and small children, for example—were sometimes identified by court officials by given names or with the descriptive term "wife."

As migrants to the New World, whatever the circumstances of their transfer may have been, the blacks forged a new culture upon their arrival in Virginia, a system of ideas, assumptions, and beliefs based in part upon a remembered African past but equally informed by the demands of an unfamiliar physical and social environment. In fact, for all mid-century colonists—black and white—resettlement involved not only an effort to preserve Old World traditions, but also a creative response to strange surroundings. The cultures formed on the Eastern Shore, therefore, developed out of an amalgam of experiences, past and present, and the end product was neither thoroughly African nor English, but uniquely Afro-American and Anglo-American.[4] The character of the blacks' background obviously is a matter of considerable importance, and though the evidence bearing on this question is sparse, some suggestive materials have survived.

Some blacks came to Virginia from the West Indies rather than directly from Africa. At the turn of the century, a Chesapeake planter, Edmund Jennings, explained to the Board of Trade that "some ancient Inhabitants" informed him "that before the year 1680 what negros were brought to Virginia were imported generally from Barbados for it was very rare to have a Negro ship come to this Country [Virginia] directly from Africa."[5] Although Jennings's informants neglected to tell him about commercial connections with New Netherland, his report was largely correct. Before Bacon's Rebellion slave traders sold their cargoes in the Sugar Islands at a great profit and thus, had no incentive to supply Chesapeake planters with all the black laborers they desired.[6] Nevertheless, for those blacks who traveled this route, Barbados played an important role in the process of cultural adjustment. While the "ancient Inhabitants" did not state how long Virginia's early slaves lived in the Sugar Islands before transferring to the mainland, it was long enough to "season" the migrants, to expose them to an alien disease environment.[7] No doubt, the Virginia planter who purchased a Barbadian slave assumed that the investment would not be lost after a single summer in the tobacco fields. Moreover, if the blacks remained on Barbados for a year or two, they learned some English. An Anglican minister, Morgan Godwyn, who toured the plantation colonies in the 1670s, observed that the blacks on Barbados spoke English "no worse than the natural born subjects of that Kingdom."[8] No record links the free blacks of Northampton to Barbados, but as we shall discover, their success in dealing with planters and their apparent good health indicated that before arriving on the Eastern Shore, they had acquired a knowledge of English and been exposed to New World diseases.

The appearance of Portuguese surnames like Ferdinando, Francisco, and Rodriggus in Northampton documents suggests, of course, that Barbados was not the planters' only source of black labor. At mid-century the obvious suppliers were Dutch merchants operating out of New Amsterdam. The Dutch-Portuguese connection went back several decades and involved a fierce struggle for the mastery of the richest colonies on three continents, Africa, Asia, and South America. The Dutch seizure of major Portuguese trading posts along the coast of present-day Angola and Zaire took place between 1641 and 1648. These slaving stations may well have been places from which Rodriggus and the other

free blacks originated. When the Dutch briefly conquered northeast
Brazil (New Holland) in the late 1630s, their interest in the slave trade
expanded, and they transported thousands of Angolans to the New
World. Some of these men and women eventually found their way to
New Netherland.[9]

The background of these particular blacks, especially their experience in the Dutch colony, is central to the story of race relations on the
Eastern Shore. Edmund Scarborough imported slaves into Northampton from New Amsterdam, and the Colonel's commercial transactions
coupled with the incidence of Portuguese surnames among the county's
free black population indicates that the migration from Angola through
New Netherland shaped the black culture of Northampton in important
ways.[10] According to the historian Charles R. Boxer, these Angolans
"practised shifting cultivation and the rotation of different crops. They
knew how to work metals, including iron and copper, and they were
fairly skilled potters. They wove mats and articles of clothing from raffia
tissues or palm-cloth. . . . They had domesticated several animals—
pigs, sheep, chickens and in some districts cattle—though they did not
use milk, butter, or cheese." The Angolans also showed dexterity in
using the hoe and the axe.[11] This familiarity with a relatively advanced,
mixed agricultural system explains in part why during the late sixteenth
century the Portuguese regarded Angola and the Congo as crucial suppliers of slave labor. Men and women with these diverse skills made excellent plantation workers, and it is not surprising that those migrants
who became free planters in Virginia did quite well for themselves. Indeed, they were probably better prepared to meet the challenge of farming on the Eastern Shore than were many white servants who came
from London or other urban centers in England.[12]

The unusual social environment of New Amsterdam shaped black
aspirations and assumptions. The Dutch colony contained a large black
population, about 700 out of 8000 persons living there in the early
1660s. Contrary to what one might expect in a colony governed by a
nation so deeply involved in the slave trade, the relations between the
two races in New Netherland was relaxed. Many blacks, of course, were
slaves. But numerous African migrants also became freemen. According
to historians of New Netherland, these free blacks encountered little discrimination, and while this assessment may exaggerate, it was possible
at mid-century for a white woman to indenture herself to a free black
for a year. Under the Dutch, freemen formed a small community,

purchased land, and established families. The names of some New Amsterdam black planters again suggest a strong cultural link with the Portuguese in Africa. Paulo d'Angola, Simon Congo, Anthony Portuguese,
and John Francisco were just a few members of this group who appeared in municipal records.[13] Nevertheless, we should note that the
black men and women who passed through the Dutch settlement, no
matter how briefly, learned that they could acquire property under certain conditions, and so instead of having their creative energies sapped
by back-breaking plantation labor in New Holland or Curaçao, these
people focused their attentions on developing personal economic opportunities. The trip to New Amsterdam was fortuitious, but once there,
the Angolans found an atmosphere in which to employ the considerable
skills they carried from the Old World.

All the blacks who arrived in Northampton came as slaves.[14] Their
situation demanded not that they wait patiently until the end of their
contracts, but rather, that they develop strategies to escape permanent
bondage—a much more difficult challenge than that confronting the
indentured servant. There were a number of different ways by which a
black person might gain freedom—manumission and self-purchase
being the most common. Charitable masters sometimes emancipated
slaves, but such acts of generosity were both rare and unpredictable. It is
not surprising, therefore, that blacks bent on achieving freedom turned
to self-purchase, a complex agreement that allowed a slave literally to
buy his own liberty. This strategy presented extraordinary problems,
even when a master cooperated, but however formidable the odds it at
least gave the slave an element of control over his own future. Indeed,
most Northampton blacks who attained freedom did so entirely through
their own efforts, and as the county court records demonstrate, successful self-purchasers possessed a combination of tenacity, guile, ambition,
toughness, and luck.

Self-purchase obviously operated to the master's advantage. Otherwise, the system would not have developed. The key to understanding
self-purchase is productivity, for while the great planters of the Eastern
Shore required able fieldhands, all they could afford, they obviously did
not want people who were lazy or disobedient. There was the rub. For
the slave, the incentives to diligence were quite limited. He had no personal stake in increasing profits; coercion or the threat of it seldom
transformed idlers into efficient workers. One answer to the master's perennial problem was to hold out the possibility of freedom. Such an

offer provided the slave with a powerful goal, a dream, a reason to sacrifice, and even though the terms of some freedom agreements appear grossly exploitive to the modern observer, they were welcome bargains to persons who otherwise faced lifelong bondage.

Self-purchase invariably demanded substantial quantities of tobacco. If masters had forbidden dependent laborers to work for themselves, it would have been impossible for slaves to enter into freedom agreements. It was not unusual, however, for great planters to allow servants or slaves small plots of land, and according to John Hammond, laborers customarily tended their crops on Saturday afternoons and other free moments. "There is no Master *almost*," Hammond explained, "but will allow his Servant a parcell of clear ground to plant some Tobacco in for himself, which he may husband at those idle times he hath allowed him." The crucial word here is "almost." Some masters apparently restricted the economic opportunities available to their workers, and it was an element of serendipity whether a slave found himself on a plantation which encouraged individual initiative. In any event, Hammond estimated that an industrious person could save enough animals and tobacco to enable him "to live gallantly" as a freeman. While Hammond exaggerated the amount of resources a dependent worker could accumulate, it was possible to make remarkable gains.[15] In fact, several blacks did quite well. The estate inventory of Bridgett Charlton, for example, contained credits for "the two Negroes Crops in the year 1658 . . . 1220 [pounds of tobacco] . . . the two Negroes Crops in 1659 . . . 2155 . . . the Negro Mens Crops in 1660 . . . 1380." This woman sold the harvests of her slaves and faithfully recorded what they had produced on their own time. In 1655 the Northampton court learned that Charlton owed "her Negro man his share of the Cropp 4 hogshead of tobacco . . . 1373," a sizable debt for anyone on the Eastern Shore.[16]

Few men in Northampton faced as many obstacles in achieving freedom as did Francis Payne. But then, few inhabitants possessed his perseverance. Payne's saga began on May 13, 1643, when he signed and recorded several agreements with his owner, Jane Eltonhead, wife of a wealthy Maryland planter, William Eltonhead. At the time Payne was a slave. The first document began innocuously, "I Jane Eltonhead . . . covenant and agree to and with francis payne my Negro Servant (hee being parte of the Estate belonging to my children) as followeth." She assigned him the entire crop of tobacco he was then cultivating, providing that he go about his business "quietly." All decisions concerning the crop—when to harvest, for example—were left to Payne. On his side, Payne agreed to compensate Eltonhead for the use of her land and possession of the tobacco "fifteene hundred pounds of tobacco: and six Bushels of corne att the ende of this present croppe."[17] This simple covenant takes on greater significance when juxtaposed with a second contract signed that day between Payne and Eltonhead. This document indicates that Payne intended to use the profits derived from the sale of his tobacco crop to finance what we presume to be the most important purchase of his life. In exchange for his own freedom, Payne promised "to pay to my mistress Three Suffict men Servants betweene the age of fifteene and Twenty four [years] and they shall serve for six yeares or seaven att the Least, And that I francis am to paye [for] those Servants [with] the next cropp. . . . And that I Jane Eltonhead am to free the said francis (on the present after the performance of these contracts)."[18] This was an extraordinary bargain, one that might cause the historian to question Payne's sanity were it not known that he succeeded in fulfilling the contract. As a slave, he brazenly calculated that he could make enough profits to buy three white servants.

Payne accepted the challenge, and though it took longer to fulfill the agreement than he anticipated, he ultimately gained his freedom. The details of his financial dealings with William and Jane are somewhat hazy, but the Northampton records reveal that by the end of the decade Payne had delivered several indentured servants to his masters. On March 9, 1649, William Eltonhead signed a document before the county court that acknowledged having "taken bill of Mr. Peter Walker merchant for Two men servants which is for the use of francis payne Negro towards his freedom."[19] And two years later, Eltonhead affirmed that Payne was still working to achieve his dream: "Received by mee William Eltonhead gent of francis payne Negro the quantity of Sixteene hundred and fifty pounds of Tobacco and Two Servants (accordinge to the bond . . . between him and his mistress)."[20] Perhaps the planter agreed to accept the 1,650 pounds of tobacco in place of the third servant. This would have been exactly the amount that a master would have expected to pay for a seasoned hand.[21] It is illuminating that no one seems to have been bothered that a black slave purchased indentured servants to obtain his own liberty.

But Payne was not finished. His own freedom presumably meant little as long as his family remained in slavery, and no sooner had he purchased himself than he started saving for the liberty of his wife and children. On November 7, 1656, Payne's long quest came to a successful conclusion. Jane Eltonhead appeared before the local justices to "discharge Francis payne Negro of all debts, claimes or demands whatsoever, and doe this daye acknowledge to have received of the said francis payne Negro the sume and quantitye of Three Thousand Eight hundred pounds of tobacco." The following day she reiterated that she had "received full satisfaction of Francis payne of Northampton . . . Negro, for the freedom of himselfe, his wife and children." After thirteen years of labor, Payne had become in the fullest sense a free planter.[22]

Emanuel Driggus displayed similar resolve during the extended process of securing freedom for various members of his family. Like many Northampton blacks, Driggus's surname (also written Rodriggus) suggests that he had been originally enslaved by the Portuguese. His initial appearance in the Eastern Shore records occurred on May 27, 1645.[23] On that day he signed an indenture with his master, Captain Francis Pott, who was "newly come over the Baye, with some servants (whereby to make a cropp)."[24] The covenant guaranteed the freedom of two of Driggus's daughters, Elizabeth and Jane, after lengthy periods of service. Pott informed the local justices that he had "taken to service two Daughters of my Negro Emanuell Drigus to serve and to bee with me . . . the one whose name is Elizabeth is to serve thirteen yeares which will be compleat and ended by the first day of March in the yeare of our Lord God One thousand six hundred and fifty eight, in which time she will be . . . only sixteene yeares of age (or there abouts) And the other child whose name is Jane Driggus (beinge about one yeare old) is to serve . . . untill she arrive to the age of Thirty yeares old (if she soe long live) which will be complete and ended in the yeare of our Lord God one thousand six hundred Seventy and Five." Driggus was particularly concerned about his daughters' physical and spiritual wellbeing, and he made Pott promise "to give them sufficient meate, drinke, Apparall and Lodginge And to use [his] best endeavor to bring them up in the feare of god and in the knowledge of our Savior Christ Jesus etc." Curiously, while he and Pott referred to these girls as "daughters," they were not in fact Driggus's natural children. As Pott explained, "I doe further testifye that the Eldest daughter was given to my Negro man by one who brought her upp by the space of eight yeares, And that the younger he bought and paid for to Capt. Robert

Shepard."[25] Driggus and his wife Francis were subsequently sold to Roger Booker and then to Stephen Charlton. Despite these moves, however, Driggus maintained strong ties with Francis Pott, still the master of Driggus's children. On May 24, 1652, Driggus and Pott signed a second agreement involving the black man's younger daughter, Jane. Pott informed the members of the county court that Driggus had given him "Satisfaction and full payment for and in consideration of the present freedome of Jane Driggus."[26] The girl who was only eight years old thus gained her freedom twenty-two years earlier than she would have by the former indenture, and she presumably moved into the home of her adoptive black parents.

Despite heroic efforts to purchase the freedom of all his children, natural and adopted, the task ultimately proved too much for Driggus. He acquired new dependents faster than he could provide for their liberty, and sometimes he and his wife watched helplessly as members of their family were sold into permanent bondage. On December 13, 1657, Pott—one of the more solicitous masters on the Eastern Shore—informed the Northampton court that he had "bargayned, sold, assigned and sett over into Henry Armitradinge his heirs . . . one Negro Boye named Edward Drigg[u]s about three or foure years old . . . to possess . . . said Negro Boy for the whole life of the said Boy."[27] A decade later John and Hanna Webb sold to William Kendall for 6500 pounds of tobacco "one Negro woman called by the name of Ann Rodriggus aged eighteene yeares or thereabouts." The contract described the period of her service as "for ever."[28]

Another Northampton black, William Harman, purchased his freedom for 5000 pounds of tobacco—an immense sum in light of annual production figures of 1500 pounds per laborer.[29] But like Payne, Harman accepted what seemed an impossible challenge. On January 30, 1660, he signed a complicated freedom agreement with William Kendall, one of the leading planters of the county. This document graphically reveals the obstacles that confronted the ambitious slave. Kendall agreed to "oblige my selfe . . . that after the Expiration of two Complete yeares from the date hereof, that if the said Negro man [Harman] put mee in goode and Sufficient Security, for the payment of five thousand pounds of tobacco and Caske clear of grounde leaves or trash, within two Complete years after, vizt. two thousand five hundred pounds of tobacco and cask each year, att some Convenient place in that County of Northampton by the bay side, that then the said

Negro to bee a free man." The great planter had just paid William Sonart "four thousand pounds of good tobacco and Caske" for Harman.[30] Thus, in addition to gaining two years of the black man's service, Kendall stood to clear a profit of 1000 pounds of tobacco. And of course, given the herculean dimensions of the task, Kendall may well have reasoned that Harman would never succeed. If the planter had such thoughts in mind, he surely underestimated the powerful incentive that freedom presented to the enslaved.

Other masters wrote freedom agreements to suit the peculiar needs of their own plantations, sometimes requiring the slave to deliver up a certain quantity of tobacco, an indentured servant, or both. In January 1649 Captain William Hawley presented two blacks, Mingo and Phillip, with an opportunity to purchase their freedom.[31] At the time these two men apparently owed Hawley's friend John Fisher four years' service. If they performed this work "faithfully and fully"—again the goal of these contracts provides an incentive to greater efficiency—they would earn a chance to be "free men and labor for themselves." Phillip and Mingo agreed to produce "the Sume of Seventeen hundred pounds of tobacco and caske," or if they preferred, "one Manservant, beinge an able hand."[32] Another black living on the Eastern Shore entered into a similar agreement, but judging from the Northampton court records, he had trouble meeting his master's stiff demands. The local justices noted in the early 1650s that John Gossall had promised John Watkins a thousand pounds of good tobacco, "And more, one sufficient able woman Servant [with] four years tyme to serve, no parte thereof yet Satisfied."[33]

In several cases it is impossible to reconstruct exactly how an individual achieved liberty. In the early 1650s, for example, Philip Mongum warned the colonists of the Eastern Shore of an impending Indian attack, and in all probability, he owed his freedom to this timely piece of intelligence.[34] Anthony Longo became a free man in 1635, but this fact was not formally recorded until the summer of 1640 when his former owner, Nathaniel Littleton, read a sworn statement to the other members of the Northampton court. Littleton declared that "by a certen wrytinge under my hand," he "really and Freely acquitted, discharged, released, and sett Free him the said Anthony Longoe From all service and servitude whatsoever from the Beginning of the World untill that present day." It is not clear what Longo had done to obtain freedom, but Littleton mentioned the fulfillment of "certen considerations."[35]

Occasionally, the name of a free black planter would simply appear in the Northampton documents, and the absence of background materials suggests that some freedom agreements were either lost or never recorded. A few blacks seem to have gained their freedom after promising to serve an especially long period of time, and for reasons that remain obscure, their masters did not demand money, tobacco, or servants in exchange for liberty. In 1648 the wealthy planter Stephen Charlton, announced in open court that "Jno Hamander Negro, his servant, shall from the date hereof serve the said Mr. Charlton . . . until the last day of November which shall be in the year of our Lord . . . one thousand six hundred Fifty and eight and then the said Negro is to bee a free man."[36] Charlton may have viewed the promise of freedom as a means of fostering greater productivity; he may have disliked the institution of slavery. Whatever his reasoning, he received several more years of service from Hamander than he would have obtained from a white servant. Charlton offered the same terms to John Eomand, also listed as a "Negro."[37] In that year the great planter likewise recorded an agreement regarding Susanna Grace, then only three years old. He assigned "all my right and title of my Negro child . . . by the name of Grace-Susanna to mr Richard Vaughan . . . the said Negro child [to serve Vaughan] till she be of the age of thirty yeares and att the end and expiration of which tyme [the] said Richard Vaughan or his heires or assignes is to sett her free which will be in the yeare one thousand Six hundred seventy-five; and likewise the said Richard Vaughan . . . is to bring the said child upp in the feare of god and to allow her sufficient Food and Cloathinge."[38]

These remarkable blacks possessed certain attributes, ambition, energy, perseverance, the very traits that enabled men like Edmund Scarborough and Obedience Robins to rise to the top of Northampton society. In this environment filled with persons looking for the main chance, exploiting opportunities before disease or violence cut them down, the winners displayed a single-minded ability to acquire property. Material goods were the basis of power, respect, and freedom and, even as slaves, Payne and Harman understood this social and economic calculus. Without property the great planters were transformed into common farmers, the free blacks reduced to dependent laborers. As anthropologist Sidney Mintz explained with reference to the blacks of the Caribbean, "The slaves sought desperately to express their individuality through the acquisition of material wealth. . . . Torn from societies that had not yet entered into the capitalist world, and thrust into settings that were profoundly capitalistic in character on the one hand, yet rooted in the need for unfree labor on the other, the slaves saw liquid capital not only as a means to secure freedom, but also as a means to attach their paternity—and hence, their identity as persons—to something even the masters would have to respect."[39] This observation was as true for Northampton as it was for the Sugar Islands.

The free blacks of Northampton could never take their freedom for granted. Self-purchase—however arduously achieved—represented but a single benchmark on the road to becoming a free planter. Full independence demanded access to land, the only certain means of gaining self-sufficiency in this agrarian society. The record of the blacks in obtaining acreage was impressive. They acquired land through leasehold agreements as well as direct purchase. Emanuel Driggus did particularly well for himself. By carefully expanding the size of his herd of cattle, he built up resources sizable enough by the mid-1660s to acquire a profitable leasehold. He negotiated an arrangement with William Kendall for 145 acres on Kings Creek in Northampton (see map). Driggus held the rights to the land for ninety-nine years and in return, he paid Kendall a total price of 7500 pounds of tobacco. To finance this deal, Driggus sublet a 50-acre section to a white tenent. According to the country records, "Now Know yee that I the said Manuell Rodriggus and Elizabeth Rodriggus for and in Consideration of two thousand five hundred pounds of Good Tobacco and Caske in hand to Content Received, have Covenanted, agreed, leased, and Lett to farme fiftie Acres of the above said parsall of Land up in the woods towarde old plantation Creeke . . . unto Bartholomew Cozier . . . for and duringe the tearme of Eighty and Seven yeares."[40] As this legal description indicates, this land was located on the southern side of Driggus's plantation, away from the water, and therefore, it was the least valuable part of the Kendall leasehold. The Cozier contract reduced Driggus's expenses to 5000 pounds of tobacco, a significant reduction for a man so busy trying to purchase his children's freedom. In April 1672 Driggus exchanged part of the Kendall property for a leasehold of 100 acres from John Waterson, a well-to-do planter who lived at the head of Kings Creek. The contract stipulated that Driggus would receive "One hundred Acres of Land lying and being in the County of Northampton . . . upon the Bay side . . . for the time of ninty nine [years]." The documents connected with this transfer provide a detailed description of Driggus's former holdings.

He had built up a large farming operation that included the "Messeague [messuage] or Tentement together with Ninety five Acres of Land being part of [the] One hundred forty and five acres of Land . . . with all houses, outhouses, orchards, gardens and apputenances." Driggus also assigned to Waterson "all Rents fines or proffits" due from Cozier.[41] Why this former slave traded a well-established farm for open land lower down on Kings Creek is not known, but the new location afforded easy access to the water, a crucial consideration to any tobacco grower. And perhaps even more important, he held this leasehold free of debt.

Another free black, Tony Longo, and his wife had accumulated sufficient resources by March 1655 to purchase a large freehold, a farm of at least 250 acres.[42] And Philip Mongum also managed to become a relatively prosperous tenant farmer. He may have cultivated a leasehold as early as the mid-1660s, but the records on this point are ambiguous. In any case, in 1678, Mongum and two white men, Edward Parkinson and Peter DuParks, leased a 300-acre plantation from Mary Savage. This land was located on Mattawaman Creek about a third of the way up the Virginia Eastern Shore. It is not certain whether the three men divided their plantation into equal shares. Whatever the nature of their partnership may have been, Mongum quickly doubled his holdings. In 1680 he acquired a 200-acre leasehold on a small creek near the Virginia-Maryland boundary.[43]

Because the county clerks of Northampton seldom bothered to record the location of a person's dwelling, it is difficult to ascertain exactly where all the free blacks lived. What evidence is available suggests that they did not hive together. The large Johnson family, discussed in a separate chapter, centered in the vicinity of Pungoteague Creek, an area later incorporated into Accomack County (see map). Philip Mongum cultivated tobacco on his Mattawaman Creek plantation before moving some forty miles north to a farm near the Pocomoke River. Francis Payne lived thirty miles to the south of the Johnsons on Cherrystone Creek, while the Drigguses owned land on Kings Creek near the southern tip of the Eastern Shore.[44] Dispersion meant that in their everyday affairs black planters regularly came into contact with white men and women, neighboring farmers who paddled along the same tidal streams and who met while gathering wood and chasing hogs. On the other hand, these people were not isolated from other black planters. As we shall discover, they maintained commercial and social relations even though the trip from Pungoteague Creek to Cherrystone Creek, for example, required considerable time and effort.

Free blacks supported their families through a myriad of agricultural pursuits, with tobacco cultivation always preeminent. These people were fortunate that tobacco was the major crop on the Eastern Shore, for while it demanded constant attention—hoeing, topping, suckering—it required a relatively modest outlay of capital. The grower did not require access to a large piece of machinery like a sugar press, which only the wealthiest planters could have afforded. Indeed, after the land was cleared, a man could immediately begin to set out plants. The rest was physical toil. To make a crop of 1900 pounds of tobacco, a bountiful harvest during this period, a farmer had to put out approximately 10,000 seedlings over two or three acres.[45] Black planters, like their white neighbors, did as well as the weather and soil allowed. In a few cases when self-purchase was the goal, they achieved spectacular results. They certainly produced enough tobacco to pay substantial fines from time to time. In 1672 the court fined Driggus 450 pounds of tobacco. Payne ran up a debt of 500 pounds of tobacco, while in 1674 the Northampton justices ordered Mongum to pay John Parker an old debt of 2500 pounds of tobacco.[46]

The prosperity of Northampton's free blacks also depended heavily upon their success in raising livestock. Cows and pigs multiplied rapidly in this environment, and with reasonable care, a farmer might build up his holdings quickly. Certainly, during the middle decades of the seventeenth-century, cattle—and to a lesser extent hogs—were the best investment an ambitious planter could make.[47] Emanuel Driggus understood this reality as well as any of his contemporaries. In fact, he began to develop a herd well before he had gained his liberty. One day, while still a servamt, he was challenged by someone who evidently refused to believe that a black could possibly legally own such an impressive number of cows, pigs, and chickens. Fortunately, his master, Francis Pott, came to Driggus's defense, assuring the members of the county court that "Emanuel Driggs and Bashasar Farnando, negroes, now servants . . . have certain cattle, Hoggs and poultry now in their possession . . . which they have honestly gotten and purchased in their service formerly under the said Capt. Pott and since augmented and increased under the service of Captain Stephen Charlton." Both planters, Charlton and Pott, swore that these animals "with their increase" were the property "of the above said Negroes and that they may freely dispose of them either in their life tyme or att their death."[48] The incident revealed not only the two blacks' skill at animal husbandry, but also the danger that unscrupulous Virginians would attempt to strip them of their rightful patrimony.

Once he had become a freeman, raising livestock continued to be Driggus's principal source of income. Buyers, both black and white, sought him out, for he was apparently recognized as one of the better horse breeders in the county. Early in 1660 he sold Alexander Wilson "one Mare coult [colt] collard Grey" for "good and valluable Satisfaction." On another occasion he provided "Sandoe the Negro" with a black heifer "for him and his heirs for ever." It may have been that Sandoe was attempting to start a herd of his own, the basis of some future freedom agreement. The profits that Driggus made from these transactions were considerable. In one memorable sale, William Kendall gave Driggus 2000 pounds of tobacco in exchange for a young mare.[49] Francis Payne and Philip Mongum were less involved in horse trading than was Driggus, but both men also endeavored to raise a variety of livestock on their plantations. In June 1655 Payne purchased from John Corneliuson, a local merchant, "one Mare, colored Baze." Within a few years, Payne sold this animal's "Mare coult" to Anthony Johnson for over 2000 pounds of tobacco.[50] Like other free blacks, Philip Mongum calculated his financial success in terms of livestock. Each horse represented a considerable investment, and when a "light bay mare" disappeared in July 1678, Mongum searched frantically for the lost animal, rightly suspicious, one suspects, that it had not simply wandered off on its own. He appeared before the Northampton court to post a reward for anyone bringing it back.[51] Unhappily, it is impossible to determine whether this device worked, for the records never again mention Mongum's prized "light bay."

Most blacks displayed similar eagerness to obtain cattle. In fact, livestock transactions of this type brought black planters before the county justices more often than did any other form of business. Anthony Johnson was an especially active buyer. On May 8, 1967, John Pott of Magothy Bay sold Anthony's son John "one Cowe calfe aged about two months." The distance between Pott's plantation and Pungoteague Creek was well over forty miles by water. In January 1648 James Berry sold Anthony "one Cowe calfe," and just a month later "Edward

Douglas . . . sould unto Anthony Johnson one yearling heiffer for . . . [a] Sume already in hand." Later that year, the Northampton clerk recorded John Winbery's sale of a "red Cowe" to Johnson. In July 1654 "William Stringer of the County of Northampton [did] . . . make sale unto William Harman of the aforesaid County, Negro—one Cow Calfe."[52] This extensive cattle trade brought free blacks into contact with a large number of white planters whom they normally could not have expected to meet. In other words, these animals provided more than a highly profitable investment, more than a means to ensure financial independence. They became the basis of a complex transactional network involving many persons scattered widely over the Eastern Shore.

However, within the black communities themselves the family was the central institution. It provided an opportunity to become fully human, to give and receive affection, to express intimate thoughts, to achieve a measure of security in an otherwise frenetic environment, to consider a future that included children as well as grandchildren. It was, in fact, a vehicle for the transfer of culture from one generation to the next. The vitality of these units may surprise those who assume that Afro-American family life was attenuated during most of the seventeenth century. Some historians have pointed out that there were relatively few black women in the region, and without the possibility of stable marriages one would not expect to find a well-developed family structure.[53] But for reasons not altogether clear, the Northampton blacks present a notable exception to this general description. The sex ratio of the Eastern Shore blacks was remarkably balanced. Of the 101 blacks who appeared on the tithable lists between 1665 and 1677, forty-eight were women and fifty-three men.[54] This balance made it easier for the free blacks to find marriage partners. Anthony and Mary Johnson lived together for almost half a century, miraculously surviving Indian attacks, contagious disease, and plantation fires. Their sons found wives, and these couples in turn bore a new generation of Johnsons. Emanuel Driggus was married first to Francis, and after she died, to Elizabeth. Francis Payne married a white woman, Aymey, and in his will written early in 1673, he gave "unto my lovinge wife . . . my whole Estate [moveables and] unmovables, making her my . . . exectrix." Sebastian Cane and Grace, Philip Mongum and Mary, John Francisco and Arisbian, all were married free black couples. Tony

Longo had a wife, although the records fail to reveal her name. No doubt, there were other pairs who for one reason or another never appeared in the court's files.[55]

We know little about courtship patterns, although one engaged couple did leave a detailed account of their negotiations on the eve of marriage. Jane Gossall, widow of John Gossall, free black planter, insisted that her intended husband, William Harman, draw up a written contract stating some of her rights after she became his bride. This is a particularly instructive document, one of the few marriage agreements that we possess from the seventeenth-century Eastern Shore. Behind the formal legal phrases in the court book, one finds a young man's impatience to get on with the ceremony. "All men shall know by these presents," he declared in the spring of 1666, "that I William Harman of the County of Northampton in Virginia, Negro, do hereby binde my self, my Heires . . . to pay and deliver unto Jane Gossall, Negro woman of the same County . . . one sufficient Mare Colt by the tenth day of October Anno Dom; 1668." She had apparently given him something for the horse, "full Satisfaction" according to the records. And then quite unexpectedly, Harman explained, "I *suddenly* Intend to make [Jane Gossall] my Lawfull married Wife." The word "suddenly" leaps from the page. Perhaps Jane Gossall had recently learned that she was an expectant mother. Whatever the situation, she held out for the horse, and Harman guaranteed that the "Mare Colt shall properly belong, and bee att all times and for ever att the disposal of the said Jane . . . and that it shall be Lawful for her . . . to give, sell and dispose of the said Mare Colt, and her Increase without my consent, or knowledge."[56]

Marriage, of course, involved more than taking a spouse. It introduced an outsider into another family; it broadened kinship ties. Again in the case of William Harman, his affiliation with Jane Gossall, née Driggus, connected him to the large Driggus clan. The bond between Emanuel Driggus, the aging patriarch, and Harman became particularly close. When Driggus transferred some property to his children in 1673, he made special provision for "my loving son in Law William Harman, Negro." Driggus's reference to his affection for Harman reveals that within one free black family at least, it was possible for members of different generations to develop warm working relationships.[57]

Mindful of the trials they had experienced in gaining freedom,

Northampton's free blacks displayed extreme solicitousness toward their children's economic welfare. Property, usually a cow or horse with which the child could start a herd, ensured that a son or a daughter would have a chance of succeeding. Characteristically, Emanuel Driggus made painstaking plans for his children's future. Probably because livestock had played a central role in his own escape from slavery, he sought to provide his offspring with healthy breeding stock. Appearing before the local justices, he began to transfer some of his famed horses. On September 29, 1673, he swore before the county clerk that "I, Manuell Rodriggus of the lower part of the County of Northampton, Negro, out of the Naturall love and affection I have and beare to my Two Daughters, Francy and Jane, Negroes . . . Doe freely and absolutely give and grant unto my Said Two Daughters and to their heirs . . . One Bay mare which I bought of Daniell Till, beinge foure yeares old." He specifically instructed Harman to guarantee that the horse would be used only for the "Benefitt and profitt . . . of my Said Two Daughters and their heirs." On the same day, Driggus turned his attention to the needs of two other children, a son Deborick and a daughter Mary. The father declared, "out of the Naturall love and affection I have and beare to my son and Daughter . . . [I do] freely and absolutely give and grant unto [them] . . . one black mare . . . foure yeares old last springe with all her future increase, male and female." Judging from the detail of his description, one concludes that these must have been very special animals. Driggus wanted to make certain that the correct mare was received in each case. When he made these gifts, it apparently never occurred to him that his children's world might contain fewer opportunities than did his own.[58]

Tony Longo cared as deeply about his son and daughters as Emanuel Driggus did about his. Unfortunately, Longo's misadventures and poverty, about which we shall have more to say later, deprived him of the means to express—at least in terms of property—his "natural love and affection." His story is of significance not because he failed to provide for his children's welfare, but because he never gave up the dream of creating a stable family even when the odds against him doing so were overwhelming. Longo frequently ran afoul of the law, and while the Eastern Shore justices never threatened to make him a slave (a point of no little importance), they did set about to deprive him of his children. Little is known about the early rounds of this controversy, but in 1669 Longo petitioned Governor William Berkeley "to be eased of his great charge of children." The efforts of the Accomack County court to take Longo's offspring from his custody apparently sparked this unusual request; after all, not many free blacks in the seventeenth century wrote directly to the royal governor. Berkeley, predictably enough, referred the entire matter back to the local court. The justices concluded, no doubt, that they could do whatever they pleased with this perennial troublemaker. They declared that "considering the lazy & evill Life of the said Anthony Longo and that his children are vitious and lazily bred so that they are like to prove noe better than their slothful father if continued with him." To preserve Longo's offspring from his baleful influence, the court assigned them to new homes. The "bigger girl" became an apprentice to Captain Gorge, the "youngest girl" went to Captain Edmund Bowman, and the "Boy" to none other than Colonel Edmund Scarborough. After they had reached the age of twenty-four their masters were required to give Longo's children their freedom. As objectionable as the court's actions may appear today, it is clear that the justices thought they were behaving conscientiously. The girls, they believed, should be schooled in "housewiffery, spinning, knitting, and such like," while the boy was "to bee put to shoemaking." And Longo, for reasons never explained, was excused from paying "publike taxes."[59]

Whether the court was justified in breaking up Longo's family is difficult to judge. Perhaps he was an irresponsible parent. He certainly did not think this was the case. Appalled by the prospect of losing his children, Longo again petitioned the Accomack court "desiring Liberty to Keepe his Children and not to [have them] disposed of according to the Court's order." If nothing else, Longo seems to have been well versed in legal procedures. At this point the justices relented a bit. Longo retained custody of his elder daughter, but the two younger children were sent off to their new homes. Without gainsaying the personal anguish of Longo at his loss, the most instructive aspect of this case is that the justices respected Longo's freedom enough to worry about training his children to be good craftsmen and good planters' wives, in other words, the very positions to which the free blacks aspired.

The centrality of the family in the lives of Northampton's free blacks is reflected in other, less dramatic documents. Several blacks recorded wills. These statements, often written when a man thought that death was imminent, reveal not only concern about passing property on to specific individuals, wives and children but also optimism about the future. This is a point of cardinal importance. The future and the family were closely intertwined in their minds, and while historians of the seventeenth century sometimes anticipate the coming of a full-blown slave society, the dying planter obviously could project a future based only upon his own experience. And they foresaw not a world filled with racist constraints, but a continuation of a social order containing opportunities for those people willing and able to seize them.

This was certainly Francis Payne's view. In the spring of 1673, his health failing, Payne drew up his last will and testament. The document provides considerable insight into Payne as a human being and into his relationships with his immediate family. Beginning with a reaffirmation of religiosity, he declared, "I bequeathe my Soule to my almighty father . . . and to Jesus Christ who by his blessed and perfect suffering redeemed [?] his servant . . . and for my body I bequeath it unto [?] the ground from which it came, there to return again Corporall." Even faced with death, however, Payne's thoughts were on the future, the setting up of his family; for like other planters of the Eastern Shore, he aimed to accumulate property over generations. "And as for my worldly estate," he continued, "I doe give and bequeath [it] unto my lovinge wife." Having recorded earlier wills, Payne now stated that "all former wills by me made and signed are revoked and made void." And finally, after stipulating "that [his] debts may in the first place bee paid," Payne provided for his godchildren: "it is my desire that my wife shall give unto each of our godchildren a cow and also a pigg when they attaine to lawfulle age." Whether the godchildren were actual relations or fictive kin remains unclear. One of them was in for an unpleasant surprise. Douras Drogas (possibly a form of Rodriggus) had apparently alienated his godfather, and not being one to let bygones be bygones, Payne ordered, "as for Douras Drogas, hee is to have nothing by this will." [60] It was not a good idea in the seventeenth century to cross the family patriarch, be he black or white.

Sebastian Cane drew up his will in June 1670. It showed the signs of haste, and in contrast to Payne, who wrote several wills in his lifetime, Cane avoided the matters until he became desperately ill. Faith and family occupied his thoughts during the last hours. "I, Sebastian Cane," he stated, "beinge Sick in body and of good and perfect memory (thanks be to God) Do make and declare this my last Will & Testament . . . First and above all things, I commit and comend my Soule into the hands of almighty God and Jesus Christ, my Savior, my body I comit to the earth." The second priority was the distribution of property he had accumulated as a Northampton planter. "All housing and such Transitory Estate as God hath blessed me with," Cane instructed, "All I give and bequeath unto my beloved wife Grace Cane all my Estate both in Virginia [unreadable] . . . also, whereof I Sebastian Cane have to this my last Will and Testament Sett my hand."[61]

While the overall importance of the family for free blacks is incontestable, we know considerably less about the structure and character of relations within Northampton's free black families. The evidence does allow us to hazard a few general observations. First, while Johnson, Payne, and Driggus were dominant figures, their wives were hardly passive individuals. Jane Harman more than held her own with William; Mary Johnson advised her husband during the Casor affair. Indeed, the frequency with which free black women appeared in the county records suggests they were as tough and aggressive as their husbands. Second, these families maintained close ties even after children had grown and married. The representatives of different generations may have shared tasks; perhaps they even lived together in the same household. In the Johnson family this certainly seems to have been the case. And third, the mention of godchildren in Payne's will indicates that some blacks developed an institution of ritual co-parenthood, known in Latin American countries as *compadrazgo*.[62] This device brought persons not related by blood into reciprocal arrangements. Godparents took on a responsibility for the welfare of another couple's offspring. Considering the high mortality rates in mid-century Virginia, co-parenthood may have provided security to parents who feared that they might die before their children came of age. Payne obviously treated his godchildren as if they were his natural children. And Driggus adopted two young girls, thus becoming a foster parent if not a godparent. The problem with such speculation is not the absence of rich supporting data but the danger that it may cause us to overlook an element of fundamental importance. The black families worked. Regardless of their form, they furnished the Harmans, Canes, even the Longos with a meaningful source of identity and spiritual strength.

Beyond the family, the Northampton County court was the central institution in the lives of the free black planters. This should come as no surprise. The court functioned both as a judicial body and a governing board, and at one time or other, almost everyone in the county came before the local justices. The problem, of course, is that colonial

historians have been so concerned with documenting the development
of racial discrimination that they have placed excessive attention upon
the acts of the House of Burgesses. While the representatives to the colonial assembly tended, especially after 1660, to treat black people as
lesser beings and to reduce them to slavery whenever possible, the
Burgesses did not have a significant impact before 1680 upon the character of local justice on the Eastern Shore. Certainly, it would be a mistake to assume that the free black planters only came before the county
court under duress, as victims of white harassment, or that the justices
treated them unfairly simply because they were black. As often as not,
these people initiated legal proceedings. They sued their neighbors and
were sued in return. On the whole, their record before the county court
seems neither better nor worse than that compiled by small white
planters.

One might anticipate that the Northampton justices would have
been most sensitive about violations of laws pertaining to firearms. As
Edmund S. Morgan observed, "Men with guns are not as easily exploited as men without them," and if the free blacks had presented a
special threat to the authority of the great planters, then surely the justices would have found ways to disarm them.[63] But, as we saw earlier in
William Harman's successful suit to regain possession of his gun, this
did not happen. Likewise, the experiences of Philip Mongum reveal
that the court was surprisingly tolerant of anti-social behavior, be the offender black or white. At first Mongum's career went well enough. Like
Driggus and Payne, he accumulated property, including a large herd of
livestock, and in 1651 his household possessions included "one Iron
Pott; one kettle; one frying pan and Two gunns and Three . . .
cowes."[64] The firearms stand out on this list, especially in light of his
later appearance before the Northampton justices. It was not long before
Mongum ran afoul of the law. His first recorded offense occurred in the
spring of 1660. The court "Upon Sum presumptious Susspition that
Philip Mongum, Negro, hath stoll [stolen] hoggs," ordered him to "pay
for his presumptious acts . . . one hundred pounds of tobacco and
Caske with Court Charges." Not long thereafter, one of the guns listed
on the inventory brought Mongum into a confrontation with the sheriff.
According to a deposition filed in the case, "Philip Mongum hath
imployed an Indian with a Gunn which said Indian meeting with
Walter Price in the woods did very much abuse him whereby the said
Price hath spent some time for Reparation." This statement was frustrat-

ingly brief. Apparently, Mongum armed an Indian—for what purposes is not clear—and the Indian then got into an altercation with a white planter. What caused this quarrel or what the court meant by the curiously understated word "abuse" is not known. The justices castigated the black man for "Suffering an Indian to carry his gunn in [the] woods contrary to Law." In his defense, Mongum "most humbly Submitted himselfe to [the] Court . . . and pretended his Ignorance of the Law." Despite this lame excuse and despite a prior record of criminality, the court showed Mongum demonstrable lenience. It treated the matter simply as a question of personal liability. He had to "make Satisfaction to the said Walter Price for expense of tyme, twenty pounds of tobacco per day and pay Court charges."[65] Mongum was not jailed. No attempt was made to disarm him or to punish him for arming an Indian, an offense which according to Virginia statute carried a fine of ten thousand pounds of tobacco or two years' imprisonment "without bayle."[66]

Northampton's free blacks were astute students of the local legal process. Unlike the white settlers, these people arrived on the Eastern Shore ignorant of the workings of common law. To seventeenth-century Englishmen, even those found in the lowest ranks of society, the law represented an important set of constitutional principles or rights. To be sure, an individual's knowledge of the exact nature of these principles was often shallow; but his sense of being part of a common-law tradition, his personal exposure to actual courts in the mother country, persuaded him that the law limited the arbitrary exercise of authority.[67] But this was not part of the blacks' culture. Whatever institutions of justice they knew in Africa, they learned about the common law in Virginia, and as the career of Francis Payne demonstrated, a black planter could be as litigious as any other inhabitant.

Payne's determination to utilize the county's legal institutions to his own advantage had been instrumental in his escape from slavery. Acutely aware of his own rights and not without prospects for success, he repeatedly sought legal remedy for economic grievances. In 1651, having failed to collect a debt from Joseph Stowe through non-judicial means, he turned to the court. Stowe, it seems, had purchased a heifer from the black planter, but before settling his account he moved to Maryland. Payne countered by filing suit in the Northampton court. The local justices listened while "Francis Payne, Negro . . . [presented] a debt due to him from one Joseph Stowe, Junior, an Inhabitant of Maryland, the Sume and quantity of Three hundred and ten pounds of Tobacco with Charges for which he hath Attached a Heiffer of the said Stowe in the county." After hearing Payne's testimony, the court ordered that "Judgement be enforced . . . forthwith . . . whereby the plaintiff may bee satisfied his debt with charge in the Suite." Payne obtained a new heifer and Stowe was advised that if he ever appeared on the Virginia Eastern Shore, he would stand "Legall Tryall" to discover why he had absconded in the first place.[68]

In June 1672 Payne instituted a bizarre suit against a Northampton planter and tanner named Joseph Benthall. The case revolved around the mysterious disappearance of one of Payne's hogs. The evidence—at least from Payne's perspective—pointed to Benthall as the culprit who had made off with his pig. On his part, Benthall hotly protested his innocence. Both men came before the Northampton justices, but after hearing the alleged facts, the justices ruled that the matter "is for the present Suspended until the Court may be better informed." The very next day the two planters reopened the business "concerninge a Hogg that the Said Paine alledgeth that the said Benthall hath killed belonging to him the Said Paine, which fact the said Benthall utterly deny." The subsequent testimony as well as the race and status of those called as witnesses provides a tantalizing insight into the workings of this county community on the eve of Bacon's Rebellion. Payne built his case around the declarations of two black people who worked for Benthall and who apparently had befriended Payne. The first was Bridgett, described in the records only as the "Negro Woman of Colonel John Stringer, now in the service of the said Benthall." It took courage to speak out against her master's interests, but that is exactly what she did. Bridgett reported she had been living at Benthall's plantation located at the head of Hungars Creek in "Barstyme," and had eaten "fresh porke" three days before Benthall purchased another hog from Thomas Harmanson. Indeed, she saw "the head and legg" of the first hog floured in Benthall's "powdering Tubb." And the clincher so far as Payne was concerned, "Harmanson's Hogg was unfloured." The next witness was a black man named Silcor. His testimony corroborated only part of what Bridgett had said. Obviously frightened by the situation in which he found himself, Silcor explained that "by the Invitation of Bridgett, Negro woman, he looked into the said Benthall's powdering Tubb and did see floured porke, but whereof said Benthall had it, he knows not." Silcor also informed the court that "he [did] eate part of the head of a

Hogg which was unflourd," thus establishing that there were in fact two animals slaughtered at about the same time.[69]

In his defense, Benthall declared that he "bought a Hogg of Mr. Thomas Harmanson and floured [the] head and some other parts, but for any other fresh porke at that tyme of the yeare he had none." Benthall produced no witnesses. Although the evidence seemed to support Payne's argument, the members of the court were uncertain what verdict to render. And in the end they avoided making a decision, ordering Benthall to "be bound over to the next County Court." But if one reads the other court business recorded that day, one discovers why the justices may have been confused. Harmanson, a great planter and not a person to be taken lightly, informed the court that "Francis Paine, Negro, accidently killed a Hogg of Mr. Thomas Harmanson," and he demanded the black planter to pay two hundred pounds of tobacco in satisfaction. No depositions were taken. The justices simply ordered Payne to pay a judgment to Harmanson of "one hundred fifty pounds of Tobacco and Caske," not quite what Harmanson had requested, but a victory over Payne nonetheless. Perhaps Harmanson and Benthall conspired together to undermine Payne's credibility? Perhaps Payne really did kill Harmanson's hog in an effort to recover his losses? Whatever the truth of the matter may have been, the case never again came before the county court, and nothing is known about what happened to Bridgett and Silcor. The most significant aspect of the entire exchange was Payne's expectation that he could receive a fair trial.[70]

John Johnson, Anthony's son, matched his father's success before the county court. As we have seen, Anthony Johnson petitioned the Northampton justices in June 1655 for return of John Casor, a slave illegally seized by two white neighbors. That same summer another white planter challenged John Johnson's title to a large piece of land that ran between their two plantations. Like the Parker brothers, he may have been testing the Johnsons' standing within the community. The litigation became inordinately confusing because the defendant was John Johnson, senior, a planter and joiner, who apparently took advantage of the similarity of names to claim ownership of a patent actually made out to John Johnson, free black planter. Anthony's son was not to be intimidated by his neighbor's actions. In September 1655 he complained to the court that "John Johnson, senior, most unjustly detaineth a pattent of his for 450 Acres of Land." The black man also presented receipts and other written documents supporting his assertions. After reviewing this testimony, the members of the court "ordered that the said John Johnson, senior, shall make his appearance at the next Court . . . To answer the suite of the said John Johnson, Negro; And if it shalbe proved that the said John Johnson, senior, hath wrongfully detayned the Negro his said pattent . . . then he shall paye Damages."[71]

Anthony's son evidently understood legal procedures better than did his adversary. While the case dragged on for several years—lengthy continuances were not uncommon in Northampton—the young black planter gained the backing of the county surveyor, Colonel Edmund Scarborough. The attempt to take Johnson's land from him through fraudulent means irritated this powerful Eastern Shore leader. The deception in itself did not bother Scarborough. At stake was his pride, for the great planter had personally laid out the land in question. He informed his fellow justices, "I . . . [surveyed] a pattent of Two Hundred and fifty Acres of land in great Nassawadocke, adjoining to a Necke of Land of [250 acres] granted to Anthony Johnson." According to Scarborough, the problem of ownership would not have developed had not the two men's names been identical. And "the Sherif not [being] able to distinguish whose [land] it was . . . the said Johnson, Joyner . . . pretendeth a right thereunto." The Colonel then, in typically outspoken language, laid the matter to rest: "I declare as the Surveyor who only can detect such Error that the said Johnson, Joyner, hath no relation to the above mentioned pattent, but that John Johnson, Negro, whose pattent it is and for whom the Survey was made and by his purchased rights only taken upp." John Johnson managed his case perfectly, for by making it appear that the white planter doubted Scarborough's competence as a surveyor, the black planter enlisted an important ally.[72]

During the three decades before Bacon's Rebellion, the Northampton justices showed no reluctance to accept the testimony of black planters in cases involving white plaintiffs or defendants. In one such action recorded in June 1658, the members of the court considered a "difference depending between Captain George Parker, plaintiff, and Robert Bayly, defendant, Concerninge Land." The details of this controversy need not detain us. What is interesting from the perspective of race relations was that the local commissioners declared that "the Said Land shall forthwith be Surveyed and John Robinson and John Johnson, Negro, who did help to Cary and Claim and marke the lands when the said Land was formerly surveyed shall show the marked trees to the Surveyor that shall Survey the said Lands."[73] Likewise, on December

30, 1668, the justices instructed William Harman and four other men to appraise certain cattle at the request of Robert Blake.[74] While these were not major responsibilities, they were no less demanding or important than those performed by the great majority of Northampton's small planters.

Equally revealing are those instances in which a black planter refused to cooperate with the county court. In 1655 the local justices sent a man to Tony Longo's plantation with a warrant requesting him to appear as a witness in a trial. Longo decided, however, that he had better things to do with his time, especially during the harvest season, and not only did he refuse to accept the court document he also physically abused the deputy who was trying to carry out his assignment. The black planter—in a manner reminiscent of the Wyatts' assault on the Northampton sheriff some years earlier—shouted "goe about your business, you idle Rascall." The more he thought about the imposition on his time, the angrier Longo became. "Shitt of your warrant," he fumed, "have I . . . nothinge to doe but goe to Mr. Walker [the commissioner]?" Soon his wife joined the attack "with such noyse that [the deputy] could hardly heare [his] owne words, reading the warrant to them, which when [he] had done readinge the said Tony stroke att [him] and gave [him] some blowes." No one regardless of race got away with such open contempt of authority. Longo's truculence brought sixty lashes administered over a two-day period.[75]

The court's handling of illegal sexual relations has long been regarded as a particularly sensitive index to racial attitudes. Were the justices stricter in dealing with black offenders than with white? Did the commissioners treat racially mixed sexual unions with unusual severity? If the answer to such questions is affirmative, then it would seem that the members of the court discriminated against certain people largely on the basis of color. In point of fact, however, the Northampton justices appeared little concerned about racial categories; sexual indiscretion had to be punished no matter who did what with whom. In its response to evidence of fornification, for example, the local court compiled a fairly equitable record. A case heard in November 1654 suggests that the justices did not separate blacks out for especially harsh punishment. A churchwarden testified that "Whereas there hath bine Enormityes committed by severall persons of Nandua and Pungoteaque [Creeks] (contrary to the Lawes of God and Man), These are therefore (accordinge to my oath) to informe you . . . thereof; That according to Lawe Such offenders maye receive punishment: their Names are Abraham Morgan and Ann Shawe (nowe the wife of the said Abraham) for Fornication and Adultry. Likewise Richard Johnson, Negro and Negroe woman of the Family of Anthony Johnson, Negro, for the same fact."[76]

Similarly, whites accused of fornication with blacks received the same punishment as did whites accused of fornication with members of their own race. In January 1663 the Northampton justices learned "that John Oever hath Committed the sin of fornication with Margaret Van Noss." The commissioners fined him "five hundred pounds of tobacco" and insisted he "Enter into bond according to Act of Assembly for his good behavior and pay Court charges."[77] However, in July 1658 the court compelled Charles Cumnell to "pay five hundred pounds of tobacco and Caske for Committinge . . . Ellicit Fornication with a Negro woman of Mr. Michael, and the sherrife to Collect it."[78] Indeed, 500 pounds seems to have been the standard fine for this particular crime. In September 1663 Denum Olandum "was presented for the sin of fornication with Jane Driggus [daughter of Emanuel Driggus] and being examined confessed the fact. It is therefore ordered that hee enter into bond with security for the payment of his good behavior and save the parish harmless from the said Child and pay court charges." The justices then turned to Jane Driggus, who also under questioning admitted having had sexual relations with Olandum. She too was expected to post bond for "the use of the parish as also for her good behavior and pay Court charges."[79] Likewise, in January 1667 William Sriven was formally charged with "Committinge the sin of Fornication with a Negro woman." For this dalliance the court demanded he post bond and promise to mend his ways.[80]

While the colony laws dealing with fornication sound severe, actual enforcement was often less than draconian. Some free blacks found a way to circumvent the court's effort to regulate the sexual behavior of unmarried people; they simply ignored the local justices. Although contempt of this sort usually brought severe punishment, the Northampton commissioners apparently concluded that in such matters a bark would serve just as well as a bite. Whatever the judges may have thought, Sara King, a free black woman, refused to stand trial for fornication. In November 1666, "Thomas Driggus, Negro, servant to Lieutenant William Kendall [was] presented by the . . . Grand Jury for committinge of the sin of Fornication with Sara King, Negro."[81] King failed to appear at the time scheduled for her hearing, and the justices decided that

"Sara King, Negro, the determination of her presentment is deferred to the next Court." Her response annoyed the justices. They ordered the sheriff to "take her into his custody untill she enter into bond with sufficient security for her personall appearance at the next Court."[82] In a similar proceeding recorded on March 31, 1674, the name of Mary Rodriggus "was presented by the Grand Jury for committing the Sin of Fornication." The woman took no notice of the court's action, and again, the sheriff was dispatched to bring Rodriggus before the next meeting of the county court.[83] But for all these threats, neither King nor Rodriggus ever showed up, and in the end the commissioners moved on to more pressing business.

The punishment for "Bastard Baringe" on the Eastern Shore did not depend upon the race of the offenders.[84] Indeed, all men who fathered illegitimate children were expected to pay child support. A comparison of two cases, one in which the father was white and the other in which he was black, revealed the court's consistency in dealing with this problem. In 1667 the Northampton grand jury convicted an Irish servant, John Dorman, of getting a "Negro woman" with child. For his transgression, Dorman was taken into custody "until he enter into bond with security for his good behavior with damages and costs . . . [after which] the said Dorman [is] to be discharged from his presentment."[85] The major concern for the local justices, of course, was that the guilty parties save the parish from the expense of raising an unwanted child. The financial logic did not change when the father was a free black. In 1663 John Johnson fornicated with a white servant woman who lived on a neighboring plantation, and when she became pregnant, the court arrested Johnson. Fortunately for him his wife, Susanna, stood by her husband, and she petitioned the local justices to release Johnson from the sheriff's custody. They allowed her request providing that Johnson "put in security to keep the parish harmless from a base child begotten [of] the body of Hannah Leach and shall pay and sattisfie all such damages." He also had to obtain a wet nurse and post bond for his future good behavior. Hannah Leach, who was a servant to Edmund Scarborough, escaped corporal punishment only because her master agreed to pay "1,000 pounds of tobacco" for her security. The records did not mention that John Johnson was a free black planter.[86]

Of course, the argument for equality before the law should not be pushed too far. The great planters who sat on the Northampton court recognized the racial differences that distinguished them from the John

Johnsons and Francis Paynes of the Eastern Shore. By the same token, however, the blacks were only one of several groups identified by English settlers as being outsiders, and at mid-century ethnocentrism was probably a more powerful force shaping human relations than racism. The tithable lists mentioned certain blacks by their given names only— "Nat—a Negro," for example—but before one concludes that these persons were objects of unusual discrimination, one should note that the same document contained entries for "Philip" and "Patrick" the "Irishmen," for "Tony—a Frenchman," and for "Clause—a Dutch boy."[87] What the county clerk equated, therefore, was nation of birth and race, French, Irish, and Dutch origins, on the one hand, and Negro, on the other. This system of classification should come as no surprise. The white planters of the Eastern Shore did not understand the complex ethnic divisions of Africa, and for them, Negro became a convenient generic term covering everyone from that continent. In fact, one Virginia statute passed in 1670 described black people as having "their owne nation."[88] In 1665 a Scots minister who lived on the other side of the Bay complained bitterly of "differences betwixt us and the English . . . [which cause] many disapointments in justice, both for securing states [estates?] and persons and our peace." He admitted that "many of our Country men" did well enough in Virginia, especially considering that they rose "from so mean a beginning as being sold [as] slavs here."[89]

II

Instead of searching for early signs of debasement, we should concern ourselves with discovering how the free black planters of Northampton fit into complex social networks, into separate spheres of interaction that gave meaning to their daily lives. Like other small planters on the Eastern shore, the free blacks attempted to forge links with representatives of the local gentry. These lopsided friendships were vital to the maintenance not only of prosperity but also of freedom. Without a patron in this aggressive society, a man became vulnerable, and as we have learned from the saga of the Johnson family, there were always individuals waiting for an opportunity to take advantage of a neighbor's misfortune. The great planters provided black clients with protection, especially in the courts, against such extra-legal challenges to personal well-being. Often a former master served as the free black's patron. This was certainly true of Francis Payne. He apparently feared that other planters would try to reenslave him, and after his heroic efforts to obtain liberty, he sought iron-clad guarantees for his freedom. Fortunately, Jane Eltonhead understood his anxiety. In July 1656 she agreed to post a £200 sterling bond—a sizable sum even for the wife of a great planter—to preclude any attempt to reduce the Paynes to slavery. "I the aforesaid Mrs. Jane Eltonhead," she declared before the members of the Northampton court, "accordinge to my power [of attorney] from my husband . . . oblige him, my selfe, Executors and administrators, in the penalty of Two hundred pounds sterling money, That the aforesaid Payne . . . shall be discharged from all . . . servitude [and] his child, [and] any person or persons that doth belonge to the said Payne."[90] Posting bond was a symbolic gesture. It communicated to those who coveted a worker like Payne that they would have to deal not only with a strong-willed black man, but also with a leading family of the Eastern Shore gentry.

While the precise character of Emanuel Driggus's continuing relationship with Francis Pott is obscure, he apparently likewise relied upon his original master's good will for a long period of time. Among other things, Pott provided generous indentures to Driggus's daughter, and when Driggus accumulated sufficient means to purchase Jane, the younger of the two girls, Pott was happy to cooperate. He was not compelled to do so. After all, by the time Driggus and his wife were prepared to buy Jane's freedom, they were no longer in Pott's service. Moreover, as we have seen, when someone questioned how Driggus had come into possession of certain "cattle, Hoggs and poultry," Pott and Stephen Charlton explained to the local justices that the animals were the black man's "proper goods" to be disposed of any way he pleased.[91] One cannot say that an ambitious person like Driggus would have failed to realize his dreams had he not known Pott. It is clear, however, that his friendship with this respected Northampton planter helped Driggus to remove major obstacles along the way.

Trade of various sorts also brought the free black planters into regular contact with members of the local gentry. One obtains evidence of these transactions indirectly through court records. In other words, we learn of an exchange only when something went wrong, usually when one of the parties failed to pay a debt. When there were no problems, of course, the court was not involved. It seems probable, therefore, that the trade network between the free blacks and great planters was far more extensive than we can document. On November 13, 1656, the Northampton justices ordered Francis Payne to discharge a debt of "500 pounds of tobacco" due to Phillip Taylor.[92] Like Thomas Harmanson with whom Payne clashed over the hog, Taylor was a respected leader on the Eastern Shore. Southy Littleton outranked them both. March 29, 1669, he petitioned the county court "against Francis Pane for 3,000 pounds of Tobacco and Caske and 15 pounds Sterling money due." This was a huge amount, roughly equivalent to the income that an adult male could expect to receive for four years of work. One wonders how Payne created such a large obligation. As might be expected, however, he was not discouraged by this financial burden. By the time Littleton went to court, Payne had already retired a substantial portion of the principal, and the justices instructed him to pay "Mr. Littleton the remainder of the said debt being 1879 pounds of Tobacco, and Caske and seaven pounds sterling money and pay Court Charges." The size of the debt in this case suggests both the magnitude of Payne's commercial interaction with neighboring whites and the court's expectation that he possessed sufficient resources to meet the terms of the contract.[93]

Free blacks confidently expected the gentry to purchase their goods and to give them credit. Whether the great planters of Northampton lent money or other resources at interest is not clear. Perhaps they imported manufactured goods from England and New Amsterdam that the black planters desired. In any case, Philip Mongum owed John Custis, an important officeholder on the Eastern Shore, 325 pounds of tobacco.[94] In December 1674 the court ordered Mongum to repay John Parker a debt of 2500 pounds of tobacco.[95] William Kendall bought a horse from Emanuel Driggus for 2000 pounds of tobacco.[96] In 1658 "John Johnson, Negro" appeared before the Northampton justices, claiming "of George Parker the sum of Seven thousand pounds of tobacco and Caske."[97] And even Tony Longo, the most outspoken black planter of his generation, traded with members of the Eastern Shore gentry. In 1647 he acknowledged in court that he owed Stephen Charlton "Three Hundred and Eighty pounds of Tobacco and caske."[98] A few months later, the court announced that "Tony Longo, a Negro, shall within Thirty dayes put in Sufficient Security unto Lewis White for payment [from the] next croppe of Three Hundred eighty four pounds of Tobacco."[99] On November 24, 1669, the Accomack court told Longo to pay Daniel Foxcroft 535 pounds of tobacco and an additional 785 pounds to John Richards.[100]

We may speculate on what the great planters received from these transactions. They may have regarded them simply as good business. Or, they may have reasoned that if the blacks were obligated to them through debt, then these people might reciprocate by refusing to shelter runaway slaves, by selling a few days' labor when the supply of hands ran short, or by purchasing manufactured items only from specific importers. From the surviving records we shall never be able fully to comprehend the dynamics of these relations. What is certain, however, is the importance of men like Scarborough, Pott, and Charlton in the affairs of the free black planters. These gentlemen comprised a distinct sphere of contacts. Nothing that they did for the blacks was contingent upon the character of other social networks in which the free blacks were involved, but without them, the world of the Paynes and Drigguses would have been quite different.

Within a second sphere, no less important than the first, free black planters dealt with other black men and women who lived on the Eastern Shore. The character of these relationships contrasted markedly with those that bound patron to client. The patron-client ties tended to center on economic and legal matters; they were tenuous because they linked men of vastly different standing within the community. Edmund Scarborough could have terminated his support of John Johnson, and there would have been nothing Johnson could have done about it. Not so the bonds of the second sphere. These were peer relationships, relaxed, continuing, frequently based upon kinship. To be sure, the free blacks engaged in economic transactions. On September 16, 1661, the Northampton records state that Emanuel Driggus did "sell and deliver . . . unto Joan, the daughter of Peter George . . . one black Heifer being aged three years." Like Driggus, Joan and Peter George were free blacks.[101] No doubt, Driggus turned a profit on the sale, but it is likely that monetary return was not the sole consideration in these encounters. Blacks reinforced each other; they sought each other out. As we saw, William Harman knew of the existence and the eligibility of Jane (Driggus) Gossall, another free black, and it was ties like this that makes it possible to speak of the free blacks as a distinct group within the county community.

Despite difficulties of transportation, free blacks maintained contacts at considerable distance. Francis Payne who owned a plantation on Cherrystone Creek near the southern end of the Eastern Shore sold livestock to Anthony Johnson, who lived almost thirty miles to the north on Pungoteague Creek. As we saw earlier, on January 31, 1660, Payne informed the Northampton justices, "I . . . have bargained, sould and delivered unto Anthony Johnson, Negro, a Mare coult for and in Consideration of the sume of two thousand two hundred pounds of tobacco and Caske."[102] No doubt, Payne could have found a buyer who would have paid his price closer to home, but he chose to do business with a fellow black planter, a demonstration that cultural and economic ties were often inseparably connected. On occasion, Payne's transactions with other free blacks were less pleasant. Some ended in litigation. In February 1656 the Northampton court ordered that "John Gossall, Negro, shall forthwith make payment unto Francis Payne, Negro, the sume and Quantity of one hundred fifty-five pounds of tobacco with Court charge, whereupon all bills and Accounts are ballanced: To this day."[103]

In one case at least, the bonds linking black people cut across social status as well as physical distance. Sebastian Cane, a free black planter, befriended a slave who served on a neighboring plantation. One day in 1666 this man, Francis Jigoles, ran away from his master and somehow persuaded Cane to provide sanctuary. Not surprisingly, local authorities soon discovered where Jigoles was hiding. The county court took a dim view of Cane's behavior and ordered "the sheriff forthwith [to] take Sebastian Cane into his Custody and [to] have him given Ten Lashes on his naked shoulders for his offense in harboringe and concealing said Francis Jigoles, Negro Slave." Witnesses who testified about Jigoles's hideout also accused the two blacks of dealing in stolen goods, and hearing of this, the court decided that "Cane for his offense in tradinge with said Francis Jigoles, Negro Salve, for about a bushel and halfe of Apples which [the runaway] purloyned from his master, shall suffer one month's imprisonment."[104] Cane had to post bond as well as repay the slave's owner the cost of the apples. Harboring a fugitive slave did not threaten Cane's freedom. Within a year, he apparently regained the trust of the white planters in the area, and he was able successfully to petition the local justices "to be discharged from his bond for good behavior." After three readings of the petition, no one protested, and the sheriff returned Cane's money. Nothing more was said about Jigoles or about the circumstances that briefly brought these two black men together.[105]

Most interaction between free blacks was, of course, neither dramatic nor illegal. They visited each other, gossiped, shared food and drink. It is evident from a deposition written in 1672 that William Harman and John Francisco maintained close relations. On this particular occasion, Harman was present at his friend's house when a white planter burst in demanding that Francisco make good on a promised exchange of a "yearling filly" for "Two oxen." The men quarreled, eventually taking their differences to the Northampton court.[106] The free blacks also assisted each other outside the courtroom. They could, for example, act as guarantors for another black's freedom. On May 20, 1665, Francis Pigot, a practicing lawyer and member of the Northampton court, declared that he had "sett free and Enfranchised Hanna Carta, Negro, upon good caution therefore given by Francis Paine and Emanuell Driggus, Negroes."[107] And in 1670, when Sebastian Cane recorded his will, he asked John Francisco to serve as witness, indicating if nothing else that he knew Francisco well enough to trust him. Earlier that same year, Cane's wife's petition to the county court was "confirmed by the Corporall oath of John Francisco."[108] These events coupled with other data suggest the existence of a substantial network of free blacks on the Eastern Shore. Cane, Francisco, and Payne were friends, and through Harman, Francisco established ties with the larger Driggus clan. Herman knew Payne, since that planter had regularly traded goods with Jane Harman's deceased husband, John Gossall. Payne, of course, was familiar to both the Drigguses and the Johnsons.

The clearest evidence that free blacks consciously reached out to other blacks involved children. As we learned, Emanuel Driggus adopted two black girls, and even though his resources were limited, he succeeded in securing their freedom. An even more complicated case of black adoption occurred in 1668. A central figure in the story was a slave named Thomas Driggus. There is no indication that this person was related to Emanuel Driggus, and despite their common surname, the two men may in fact not have even known each other. Whoever his kinfolk were, they probably disliked Thomas. Indeed, everyone seems to have regarded him as thoroughly obnoxious. In the summer of 1668 a number of Northampton planters, black as well as white, informed the county court that Thomas Driggus "hath very Grossly abused them." In addition, he "neglected his Master's service." The complaint received support from John Francisco, Francis Payne and his wife, Mrs. William Morris, and Colonel William Kendall, a formidable group to have arrayed against any colonist let alone a truculent slave. After hearing the testimony concerning Driggus's misbehavior, the court ordered the sheriff to give the offender "upon his naked shoulders one and twenty Lashes well Laid on for his abuse and pay Charges of Court."[109] The records failed to describe the nature of the abuse, but judging from the severity of the punishment, Driggus must have been a genuinely nasty character.

As a result of his actions, the local justices decided to remove Driggus's infant son from his custody. The boy, presumably a slave like his father, unwittingly found himself in a vulnerable position. An aggressive planter could certainly have taken advantage of the situation to obtain a valuable fieldhand for life. But that is not what happened. John Francisco stepped forward and asked the court to award him permanent guardianship over Driggus's child. The justices agreed to his request and ruled that Francisco "in whose Custody the said Child now is" could keep the boy "untill [the said child] attaynes the age of one and Twenty yeares and then to sett it free for Ever." In one stroke young Driggus gained liberty "for Ever" and a place in a stable free black home.[110]

The discrete network of human relationships provides a fundamental insight into the workings of black culture on the Eastern Shore. Colonial historians have often stated that black people living in seventeenth-century Virginia were unable either to maintain a traditional African culture or to perpetrate a distinct Afro-American heritage. This argument assumes that because of an unfavorable sex ratio, black males could not find wives and form stable families, that these men felt isolated within an overwhelmingly white society, and that they had no choice but to accommodate themselves to prevailing English custom.[111] But as the Northampton evidence suggests, this interpretation is only partially correct. To be sure, within certain spheres the blacks adopted new ways. They learned about the common law, for example, and in economic exchanges they held their own with white planters, great and small. However, on a quite separate level of interaction they developed conscious ties with other black colonists, sometimes across long distances, and while the free black planters constituted only a small segment of the county's total population, they were by no means isolated from meaningful contact with other blacks. An extensive web of friendship and kinship provided a framework in which even the colony's earliest blacks could have transmitted notions about culture.

A third sphere of interaction possessed an altogether different character. Contact with the county's non-gentry whites, small planters and indentured servants, was a daily occurrence in the lives of Northampton's free blacks. Members of the two races exchanged land, traded livestock, worked for each other, sued one another, and socialized together. Unlike relations within the other two spheres, these neighborhood ties tended to involve no obligation of reciprocity. On this level blacks and whites dealt with each other essentially as equals. The participants were open and relaxed. In fact, during the decades before Bacon's Rebellion, economic status rather than race seems to have been the key element in determining the structure of these relationships.

As we have already discovered, men like Driggus, Payne, and Johnson traded livestock with small white planters. In fact, exchanges of this type constituted the most common form of interaction between the free blacks and their white neighbors. Sometimes, however, these relations involved more than transient business dealings. Men reached out to each other, showing exceptional compassion for the needs of another person regardless of race. Such was the case of the friendship that developed between George Williams, an English seaman, and Emanuel Driggus. According to Williams's will recorded in October 1667, the seaman found himself alone and sick in a strange country. While the man's condition was desperate, Driggus did the best he could for him, and when Williams learned that he was dying, he gave "to Manuell Driggus, Negro, for his care and trouble in tendinge mee in my sicknesse, my wages due me for Eleven Month's service on the Shipp *Louis Increase* of Bristol." In addition, the black planter received a chest full of tobacco and all the rest of Williams's possessions located in Northampton. The sailor also insisted that Driggus serve as the "sole Executor of this my Last Will and Testament." [112]

The gentlemen who served on the county court apparently assumed that the small planters were not particularly concerned about maintaining sharp racial boundaries. If a man owned property, he was a member of the community. The court did not hesitate to place a white infant in the home of a free black even though that action meant the child would be under the care and authority of black parents until it reached the age of twenty-four. On December 7, 1674, an obscure individual named Nicholas Silverdo came before the Northampton justices to answer to the charge of fornication. In standard form, the justices ordered Silverdo, "the reputed father of a bastard child . . . into the custody of . . . John Culpepper . . . High Sheriffe of the County [and] he should enter Bond to performe the same." But within a matter of months Silverdo slipped away, leaving the taxpayers of the county with an unwanted burden. It was then decided that the "child be put out to nurse with Jane Harman, Negro, the Wife of William Harman." After the Harmans had looked after the baby for more than a year, Jane Harman received payment for her services. The court instructed the sheriff to "detayne twelve hundred pounds of tobacco and caske . . . and make payment thereof unto the said William Harman for the Keeping of the said child." The Harmans could have continued this arrangement, presumably gaining a sturdy worker in the bargain, but William Harman grew tired of the responsibility of raising the child. He petitioned the court to find another foster home, "And for as much as the said Harman desired to bee discharged from keepinge the said child any longer, upon which the Court ordered proclamation to bee [made] for any person to take the said child till twenty foure yeares of age.[113]

The Harmans' experience was not without precedent. The Northampton records reveal instances of whites living in households headed by a free black. The 1668 tithable list shows one household headed by "Thomas Rodriggus, Negro," with members including, "Sara Negro, Morgan Thomas and Walter Manington," and another comprising "Tony Negro and Jack Arthur." Thomas and Manington were whites who probably worked for a black master as indentured servants, while Arthur established an informal partnership with Tony Negro to grow tobacco.[114]

Surviving documents from the middle of the century occasionally suggest the texture of daily interactions between white and black people. They also remind us of the casual violence that permeated the entire society. In May 1641 Richard Newton, a small planter, described to the members of the county court an interracial gathering at which he had been present the previous weekend. Newton stated that "upon Sonday last . . . being at the house of Anthony Longe [Longo], and John Parramore and Henery Williams being there allso," a quarrel had erupted between Williams and Parramore over several yards of cotton cloth. The men seem to have been drinking. Williams demanded the material, but the other man put him off, promising delivery or suitable substitution in due time. While Newton and Longo watched in amazement, Williams hit Parramore across the face, "and not therewith Content but againe strooke him, and swearing drew a punyard and sayd hee could fynd [it] in his heart to stabb the sayd Parramore." The court ordered Williams to beg Parramore's forgiveness for the beating, especially since it had occurred on "the Saboth day," and Parramore was given ten days to produce the cotton cloth.[115] The fact that whites had been socializing at the home of a black man did not strike the justices as noteworthy.

Philip Mongum turned his knowledge of illegal white behavior to his own profit. In 1675 he told the Northampton court that a certain John James had stolen a hog, and after a jury convicted James of the crime, Mongum demanded an informer's fee of one-half the fine which in this case amounted to 1000 pounds of tobacco. His actions probably won him no friends among the county's poorest freemen. Certainly, James may have concluded that there is no honor among thieves, for just a few years earlier Mongum had been found guilty by the same court of hog "swaggling."[116]

Black and white servants also ran away together on many occasions, as we suggested earlier. One elaborate escape attempt in 1666 revealed the close bonds that could develop between dependent laborers living on different plantations. The conspirators, a white servant and two black slaves, were the property of three separate masters. One of the owners, Lieutenant William Waters, a member of the local gentry, informed the court that "John Allworth . . . servant to Mr. John Michaell did run away with a Negro man of the said Leift Col Waters and carried away with him and spoyled severall goods of [Waters's] besides his charges in gettinge his Negro [back] againe." Waters specifically sought compensation for "17 days absence of his Negro before he had him againe." The master's careful recounting of the damages suffered makes it possible to reconstruct the course of the servants' flight. The three runaways apparently recognized that their only hope of success lay in water transport; overland travel was too slow and dangerous. In any case, an angry Waters demanded repayment for "Damage done to my Boate and oars" as well as for a large supply of food. Waters also explained to the local justices how he had persuaded neighbors to assist him in tracking down the escapees: "payd to Thomas Ball for gathering of Syder for helpinge to bringe my Negro home . . . 480 [pounds of tobacco] . . . for Richard Tull for helpinge to bringe like Negro home . . . 320."[117] For his many offenses, the Northampton County court ordered the white servant, Allworth, to indemnify Waters for the losses

and to serve an extra term of service with Waters at the end of his indenture to John Michaell. This was a stiff penalty, but long before he
took Waters's boat, Allworth must have known the legal consequences
of his actions. That he still risked flight with a black slave testifies to the
lack of racial consciousness—of at least one white servant. Moreover, in
this particular case, Allworth was accountable to a second master, John
Robins, who joined Waters in the suit against the white servant. Robins
told the court that "John Allworth . . . servant to Mr. John Michaell
did run away with a Negro of the said Mr. John Robins and [he] was att
greate charges losse and damges before he could get him againe." These
losses included "17 days of my Negro in cropp time . . . payed to
Thomas Ball for takinge of my Negro . . . 84 . . . for a Fidle . . .
100 . . . for the Losse of my Cropp . . . 500." The theft of the fiddle
was a nice touch. One hopes that the three servants enjoyed their brief
taste of freedom. From the master's point of view the runaways' most
serious crime was deserting the plantation during the harvest season.[118]

Free blacks and whites also engaged in illicit sexual relations. Like
Francis Payne and John Johnson, Philip Mongum had sexual relations
with a white woman. If any black man were capable of generating sexual anxiety within the white community, it would have been Mongum.
In point of fact, the Northampton court treated him with restraint, and
the local justices appeared more concerned about the "Sin of Adultry"
than with Mongum's color. The evidence was straightforward; Margery
Tyer bore him a child. The court ordered Mongum to "be fined five
hundred pounds of tobacco and be held in the Sheriff's Custody untill
he Enter into bond with Security for his good behavior [to] save the
parish harmless from the said child." Moreover, the court insisted that
he no longer frequent the "Company of the said Margery." Tyer fared
less well before the justices. For "the filthy sin of fornication" and bearing a "Molato bastard," she received four lashes—not a severe punishment, but more than Mongum suffered. The court warned her that additional lashes could be expected if she were caught again with
Mongum.[119]

III

After Bacon's Rebellion, the status of Northampton's free blacks deterio-
rated. To assign a precise date to such a complex phenomenon would
be impossible. The process was slow, but by the 1680s the names of sev-

eral major black families no longer appeared in the records of Virginia's Eastern Shore. Other blacks were reduced to marginal positions, legally free but without sufficient resources to hold their own.[120] While we shall probably never know exactly what caused this change in the county's social structure, two factors were clearly at work. The first was migration. From the time that Captain John Smith sailed across the Bay from Jamestown, people recognized the limited economic potential of the region. The land base was too small to support an expanding plantation society. The harbors were poor, and when Maryland's more fertile Eastern Shore opened to settlement late in the seventeenth century, many Northampton planters drifted northward, especially to desirable locations in Somerset County. This developing area offered not only better soil for tobacco cultivation but also easier access to ocean vessels than did Northampton's shallow creeks.[121] The move to Maryland involved black as well as white planters. As we have seen, Anthony Johnson and his large family took up residence in Somerset, and it was there that the patriarch's grandson established "Angola." The name Driggus also appeared in the county records about this time. In 1688 Sarah Driggus protested to the Somerset magistrates that even though she had been born a free woman, local authorities taxed her as if she were a slave.[122] The opportunity to obtain fresh land also drew Mongum north, but he may not have moved all the way to Maryland. No doubt, other free blacks from Northampton who followed the same path cannot be traced because of the destruction of local records.

A second major element affecting the status of free blacks was demography or, more precisely, an interplay between white racial attitudes and the growth of the black population. Until the 1680s the number of blacks living in Virginia remained relatively small. There were several reasons for this, not the least of which was the great planters' inability to purchase all the new slaves that they desired. At the time of Bacon's Rebellion the black population stood at approximately 2500. Soon after that, however, the number of blacks began to expand rapidly, and by the end of the century, slave traders brought several thousand blacks into Virginia each year. These men and women originated in Africa, not New Amsterdam or Barbados, and they landed in the New World utterly unfamiliar with their masters' culture or the English language. This massive influx of alien black laborers exacerbated racial tensions. It was in this period, for example, that white Virginians first openly discussed the innate inferiority of blacks. The sudden shift in the ratio of blacks to whites either generated racist ideas or brought to the surface latent racist assumptions. In either case, the final two decades of the seventeenth century witnessed a fundamental change in the character of race relations.[123]

This broad shift in racial attitudes inevitably eroded the free blacks' personal liberty. As early as 1668, the members of the House of Burgesses had distinguished this group from other freemen living in the colony. Contrary to what some Virginians apparently believed, the lawmakers insisted that the two races were not equal, and henceforth, "negro women, though permitted to enjoy their freedome, yet ought not in all respects to be admitted to a full fruition of the exemptions and impunities of the English."[124] The free blacks fell into poverty. By the end of the century, it would have been impossible for an ambitious slave to duplicate the feats of a Francis Payne, Anthony Johnson, or Emanuel Driggus. In 1699 the Virginia Assembly required every newly freed black to leave the colony within six months of manumission. They argued that without such an ordinance the free blacks would create "great inconveniences . . by their either entertaining negro slaves from their master's service, or receiving stolen goods, or being grown old bringing a charge upon the country."[125]

Local practice apparently conformed to colonial statute. The Northampton court records contain examples of free blacks becoming common criminals simply in order to survive. They were not forced out of Virginia but, increasingly, their white neighbors treated them with distrust and disdain. In 1723 a group of white planters living on the Eastern Shore complained to the Assembly that the free blacks had grown too populous. They were poor and dangerous. And in 1758 citizens from Northampton urged colonial authorities to expel *all* free blacks from Virginia. Later these petitioners compromised their demands. They changed "out of the colony" to "out of the county," but when they presented their plan to the Burgesses it was rejected without comment.[126] The free blacks remained in Northampton, but only as its pariahs.

5

Conclusion:
Property and the Context
of Freedom

Race relations in mid-seventeenth-century Northampton County cannot be understood apart from the specific social and physical context in
which they developed. The daily life of the free black planters involved
contact with a broad spectrum of people, local gentry and Native Americans, servants and slaves, and each type of interaction called forth a different response, a behavior pattern that suited the particular situation,
be it a meeting with Edmund Scarborough or a livestock exchange with
another free black. Within each sphere, one had to adopt the appropriate presentation of self, an adaptive, creative process since the context of
social transactions constantly changed, eliciting new responses. From
this perspective, race relations were defined and redefined every time
men came into contact on the Eastern Shore. In their dealings with the
great planters, the free blacks did not handle themselves differently than
a white planter or an indentured servant would have done in a similar
situation. Everyone curried the favor of the rich and powerful. Anthony
and John Johnson, Francis Payne, and Emanuel Driggus happened to
be particularly successful at finding gentry patrons, and these ties obviously served them well in their dealings with social and economic
peers. No doubt, someone like Edmund Scarborough frightened the
free blacks, but in that reaction they were not alone. Scarborough
frightened everyone. In fact, in analyzing the bonds between patron and
client on the Eastern Shore, one discovers that they were not affected by
the color of a man's skin, but by his economic status. Persons who
owned land, livestock, and slaves fared better in the search for backers

than did poorer, more marginal people, a lesson that John Casor and the Parkers learned before the Northampton County court.

In their relations with Northampton's non-gentry, the free blacks do not appear to have operated at a serious disadvantage, regardless of what Virginia statute may have decreed. In this social context they were what Edmund S. Morgan has described as black Englishmen.[1] These people showed a truculent awareness of their legal rights, and if challenged—as was Anthony Longo during the harvest season—they gave as good as they got. Black migrants who became free discovered how to employ the judicial process to their own advantage, and during the period under investigation they won as many suits as they lost. They wrote wills. They raised livestock and tobacco. They carried on an extensive trade. Whenever possible they purchased dependent laborers. They fornicated with neighborhood women, some of whom were married, some who were not, some white, some black. Indeed, if the county clerk had not from time to time inserted the word "Negro" next to their names, it would have been impossible to distinguish the Drigguses, Harmans, and Paynes of Northampton from a hundred other contemporary small planters. Within this sphere of interaction, the free blacks appear to have assimilated the dominant culture of the Eastern Shore. And again, economic status rather than racial identity seems to have been the chief factor in determining how blacks and whites dealt with one another.

But to regard these people simply as Englishmen with black skins, as persons totally absorbed into the culture of their white neighbors and former masters, would be erroneous. The free blacks were conscious of being part of a separate group on the Eastern Shore. Whether this shared identity was founded upon racial as opposed to ethnic attributes is not entirely clear. Perhaps being Angolan meant more than being black. The two elements may have been so tightly intertwined that it is foolish even to attempt a distinction. Whatever the case may have been, the free blacks reached out to other free blacks, forming a discrete network of friendships and family ties. Trade between men like Johnson and Payne merely sustained relationships based upon other considerations. And thus one can assert that within this sphere, unlike the other two, race rather than economic status was fundamental in shaping the transaction.

This interpretation avoids several problems that have plagued the literature of early American race relations. First, as the Northampton evidence demonstrates, there is no reason to depict seventeenth-century race relations in monolithic terms, as an inevitable conflict between blacks and whites. Within the specific context of the Eastern Shore, race was only one of several factors determining the character of face-to-face relations. Anthony Johnson owned a black slave; other free blacks purchased white indentured servants. Whites ran away with blacks. The interaction between the races was so great, so varied, in fact, that it makes little sense to force the data into racial categories that may be more suitable for other periods of American history. Second, the transactional approach escapes a fruitless discussion of genuine and spurious culture. It makes no sense to try to determine whether Johnson's true self was a black slave-owning Englishman or an articulate Afro-American. He was both and more. In different situations he and other free blacks adopted appropriate forms of behavior. When we analyze these complex transactions, our goal is not to determine what is "real" culture, but rather to discover "how individuals or particular categories of individuals perceive and evaluate alternative courses of action and assess their probable outcomes."[2] Seen from this perspective, culture becomes a rich personal resource helping people to adapt to an unfamiliar, changing social environment.

The experience of Northampton's black planters poignantly reminds us of the importance of analyzing men and women in the past in terms they themselves would have understood. Johnson and Payne did not think of themselves as living in a racist society. Nor, for that matter, did it occur to them that their white neighbors were making an "unthinking decision" that would reduce all black people to the lowest levels of society simply because they were black. At mid-century the world seemed full of possibilities for personal advancement. William Harman eagerly planned for his marriage. Emanuel Driggus worked diligently to place his children in this community. Free black planters recorded wills, accumulated property, and educated their offspring precisely because they believed their families would continue to play a significant role in Northampton affairs. That they were mistaken does not mean that they were foolish or naïve. Indeed, as we have seen, Johnson, Driggus, and Payne possessed shrewd judgment. Their optimism was a source of strength, and to depict them as curious aberrations in a long history of racial discrimination in America not only slights their genuine accomplishments but also assumes—quite falsely—that the story of race relations must inevitably involve degradation and exploitation.

The fact remains, however, that Northampton's free black planters did not survive. Their dramatic rise and fall merit closer examination. The foundation of liberty in mid-century Northampton—for whites as well as blacks—was property. Without land and livestock, without the means to support a family, no one could sustain freedom. Property gave men rights before the law; it provided them with an independent identity that translated into a feisty self-confidence in face-to-face contacts. Indeed, in this inchoate social system, in which people placed extreme emphasis upon personal independence, upon material gain, and upon aggressive competition, property became the only clear measure of another man's worth. And while the great planters of the Eastern Shore exploited dependent laborers, they also recognized the prerogative of almost everyone to take part in the scramble for wealth. It had not yet occurred to them to cut the Johnsons and Paynes out of the game. The free blacks rose to the challenge. Their success at building up impressive personal estates was vital to the character of daily transactions in all three spheres. Their horses and cattle cemented relations with the local gentry, helped them to hold their own in dealings with small white planters, and most important, allowed them to maintain ties with other propertied blacks without fear of harassment.

For analytic purposes it is useful to see the free blacks as a type of New World peasantry. This word has many definitions, but following the lead of Sidney W. Mintz, we employ the term *peasantry* "to refer in general to those small-scale cultivators who own or have access to land, who produce some commodities for sale, and who produce much of their own subsistence."[3] Similar groups appeared in other plantation societies throughout the Americas and, like the free blacks of the Eastern Shore, many were eventually deprived of their independence. The success of these independent cultivators was in part a source of their undoing. Northampton's free blacks competed for the same resources, primarily land and labor, participated in the same markets, and raised the same crops as did the great planters. Driggus, Johnson, and Payne were clever men, but they possessed no technological advantage, no special skill or trade that set them apart from other persons living on the Eastern Shore. This obvious point helps to explain the disappearance of the free black peasantry in this region and, for that matter, of a free white peasantry. The small planters did not establish a distinct niche in the society, an identity like that of the gypsies or the executioners in modern European societies, that might have insulated them from far-reaching social change.[4]

As in several Caribbean societies, the expanding plantation system in Virginia gradually undermined the position of the free planters. Many causes—far more than can be mentioned here—contributed to their slow destruction. The great planters achieved greater efficiency as time passed, and as tobacco prices fell over the century, they increased productivity. They secured better, more reliable relations with large English merchant houses. And most important, the local gentry acquired a steady supply of black slaves. To compete against the great planters became increasingly difficult. These powerful people monopolized large tracts of land, forcing marginal cultivators and landless freemen to leave the colony if they wanted to establish independent farms or to obtain fertile acreage to replace worn-out ground.[5] By the 1670s it would have been nearly impossible for a slave to work his way out of slavery in the manner that Francis Payne had done. The doors to economic opportunity were either shut or fast closing by that time. It was not that Payne's successors were less astute or energetic than he had been. Rather, they lost the possibility to acquire property, the basis of genuine freedom in this society.

Notes

INTRODUCTION

1. David B. Davis, *The Problem of Slavery in Western Culture* (Ithaca, 1966), 15.
2. *Ibid.*, chap. II.
3. Philip D. Curtin, "The Atlantic Slave Trade, 1600–1800," in J. F. Ade Ajayi and Michael Crowder, eds., *History of West Africa* (2 vols., New York, 1976), I, 302–330.
4. For a brief, up-to-date survey of the South Atlantic system, see, Philip Curtin, Steven Feierman, Leonard Thompson, and Jan Vansina, *African History* (Boston, 1978), 215–224.
5. Joseph C. Miller, "The Congo-Angola Slave Trade," in Martin Kilson and Robert Rotberg, eds., *The African Diaspora: Interpretive Essays* (Cambridge, Mass., 1976), 76–113.
6. Cited in Davis, *Problem of Slavery in Western Culture*, 40.
7. George M. Frederickson, "Toward a Social Interpretation of the Development of American Racism," in Nathan I. Huggins, Martin Kilson, and Daniel M. Fox, eds., *Key Issues in the Afro-American Experience* (2 vols., New York, 1971), I, 274.
8. Susie M. Ames, ed., *County Court Records of Accomack-Northampton, Virginia, 1640–1645* (Charlottesville, 1973), 457. (Hereafter cited as CCR, *1640–1645.*)

1 PATRIARCH ON PUNGOTEAGUE CREEK

1. James H. Brewer, "Negro Property Owners in Seventeenth-Century Virginia," *William and Mary Quarterly* (hereafter cited as W&MQ), 3rd Ser., XII (1955), 578.

2. T. H. Breen, "Of Time and Nature: A Study of Persistent Values in Colonial Virginia," in *Puritans and Adventurers: Change and Persistence in Early America* (New York, 1980), chap. ix.

3. Wesley Frank Craven, *The Legend of the Founding Fathers* (Ithaca, 1965), 129–133.

4. Philip A. Bruce, *Economic History of Virginia in the Seventeenth Century* (2 vols., New York, 1907), II, 126.

5. Reprinted 1969.

6. Brewer, "Negro Property Owners," 580.

7. See, Clifford Geertz, "Thick Description: Toward an Interpretive Theory of Culture," in *The Interpretation of Cultures* (New York, 1973), 3–30.

8. John Camden Hotten, ed., *The Original Lists of Persons of Quality* . . . (London, 1874), 241.

9. Alden T. Vaughan makes a persuasive case that even if these first Virginia blacks were not slaves, they held "a significantly inferior position . . . in the social structure of white Virginia" ("Blacks in Virginia: A Note on the First Decade," *W&MQ*, 3rd Ser., XXIX (1972), 476). Vaughan, however, identifies an "Antoney Negro" living at Elizabeth City in 1624 as Anthony Johnson. The Elizabeth City Antoney was married to Isabella and fathered a child named William (*ibid.*, 475–476; John H. Russell, *The Free Negro in Virginia 1619–1865*, (Baltimore, 1913), 24–25). A more solid argument can be advanced for "Antonio" of Bennett's plantation. As we shall see, Anthony Johnson's wife was Mary, a woman who arrived in Virginia in 1622, and while they had several sons, none was named William. The confusing element, of course, is the name "Antonio." There was also an Anthony located at a James River plantation, and while he may have become Mary's husband, it seems more likely that "Antonio" of Warresquioake simply Anglicized his name.

10. See, Edmund S. Morgan, *American Slavery—American Freedom: The Ordeal of Colonial Virginia* (New York, 1975), 101–102, 115.

11. *Ibid.*, 108–130.

12. Cited in Paul Fussell, *The Great War and Modern Memory* (New York, 1975), 3.

13. The fullest account of Sandys's ambitious plan remains Wesley Frank Craven, *The Southern Colonies in the Seventeenth Century, 1607–1689* (Baton Rouge, 1949), 93–137.

14. Susan M. Kingsbury, ed., *The Records of the Virginia Company of London* (4 vols., Washington, D.C., 1906–35), I, 446.

15. "Abstracts of Virginia Land Patents," *Virginia Magazine of History and Biography*, III (1896), 53–56. (Hereafter cited as *VMHB*.)

16. Richard L. Morton, *Colonial Virginia* (2 vols., Chapel Hill, 1960), I, 68, 73–76; John Smith, *Travels and Works*, ed. by Edward Arber (2 vols., Edinburgh, 1910), II, 582–583; Hotten, ed., *Original Lists*, 241.

17. *Ibid.*, 241.
18. Irene W. D. Hecht, "The Virginia Muster of 1624/5 as a Source for Demographic History," *W&MQ*, 3rd Ser., XXX (1973), 70–84; Herbert Moller, "Sex Composition and Correlated Cultural Patterns of Colonial America," *ibid.*, II (1945), 113–153.
19. See, Lois Green Carr and Lorena S. Walsh, "The Planter's Wife: The Experience of White Women in Seventeenth-Century Maryland," *ibid.*, XXXIV (1977), 542–571; Darrett B. and Anita H. Rutman, " 'Now-Wives and Sons-in-Law': Parental Death in a Seventeenth-Century Virginia County," in Thad W. Tate and David A. Ammerman, eds., *The Chesapeake in the Seventeenth Century: Essays on Anglo-American Society & Politics* (New York, 1979), 153–182.
20. Northampton County Court Records, Deeds, Wills, Etc., No. 4, 1651–1654, fol. 162 (Virginia State Library, Richmond, Virginia). (Hereafter cited as NHCR.)
21. "Isle of Wight County Records," *W&MQ*, 1st Ser., VII (1899), 283.
22. Craven, *Southern Colonies*, 234, 254–269; Morton, *Colonial Virginia*, I, 151, 171–179, 225; Jennings C. Wise, *Ye Kingdome of Accawmacke* (Richmond, 1911), 85–86, 125–128, 143–149, 164, 294; *CCR, 1640–1645*, 311; Babette M. Levy, "Early Puritanism in the Southern and Island Colonies," *Proceedings*, American Antiquarian Society, LXX (1960), pt. 1, 139–142; *VMHB*, VI (1898–99), 413–414.
23. Morgan, *American Slavery—American Freedom*, 136–140; Wesley N. Laing, "Cattle in Seventeenth-Century Virginia," *VMHB*, LXVII (1959), 143–164; Susie M. Ames, *Studies of the Virginia Eastern Shore in the Seventeenth Century* (Richmond, 1940), 51–53.
24. Brewer, "Negro Property Owners," 576.
25. This complex and often misunderstood process is explained in Edmund S. Morgan's "Headrights and Head Counts: A Review Article," *VMHB*, LXXX (1972), 361–371.
26. Ames, *Eastern Shore*, 16–42. The Johnson real estate holdings are much more impressive if we consider the lands of his two sons, Richard and John. In 1652 John presented eleven headright certificates and patented 550 acres. And in 1654 Richard obtained 100 acres, bringing the Johnson family's Pungoteague estate to 900 acres (*ibid.*, 103).
27. NHCR, Deeds, Wills, Etc., No. 4, 1651–1654, fol. 162.
28. William W. Hening, ed., *Statutes at Large* (13 vols., Richmond, 1819–23), I, 144, 292 (emphasis added); John Hammond, *Leah and Rachel, or, the Two Fruitful Sisters Virginia, and Mary-land* (London, 1656) in Peter Force, comp., *Tracts* (4 vols., Washington, D.C., 1836–46), III, 9; Winthrop D. Jordan, *White Over Black: American Attitudes Toward the Negro, 1550–1812* (Chapel Hill, 1968), 77.
29. NHCR, Deeds, Wills, Etc., No. 4, 1651–1654, fol. 205.

30. Susie M. Ames, ed., *County Court Records of Accomack-Northampton, Virginia 1632–1640* (Washington, D.C., 1954), xxxvi–xxxvii. (Hereafter cited as *CCR, 1632–1640*).

31. Ralph T. Whitelaw, *Virginia's Eastern Shore* (2 vols., Gloucester, Mass., 1968), I, 676; Wise, *Kingdome of Accawmacke*, 116–17; Nell M. Nugent, ed., *Cavaliers and Pioneers: Abstracts of Virginia Land Patents and Grants 1623–1800* (2 vols., Richmond, 1934), I, 223.

32. NHCR, Deeds, Wills, Etc., No. 4, 1651–1654, fol. 226.

33. *Ibid.*; "The Parkers of Virginia," *VMHB*, V (1897–98), 444–446; VI (1898–99), 412–413; Nugent, ed., *Cavaliers and Pioneers*, I, 185, 193, 307, 400.

34. Hening, ed., *Statutes at Large*, I, 253, 439; II, 239.

35. NHCR, Deeds, Wills, Etc., No. 4, 1651–1654, fol. 226.

36. Hening, ed., *Statutes at Large*, I, 124, 172, 197, 263, 460; Carville V. Earle, *The Evolution of a Tidewater Settlement System: All Hallow's Parish, Maryland, 1650–1783* (Chicago, 1975), 191.

37. See, Philip J. Greven, "Family Structure in Seventeenth-Century Andover, Massachusetts," *W&MQ*, 3rd Ser., XXIII (1966), 234–256.

38. Ames, *Eastern Shore*, 103.

39. NHCR, Deeds, Wills, Etc., No. 5, 1654–1655, fol. 35.

40. Morgan, *American Slavery—American Freedom*, 223.

41. NHCR, Deeds, Wills, Etc., No. 4, 1651–1654, fol. 226a.

42. "The Parkers of Virginia," *VMHB*, VI, 413.

43. See, Chapter II.

44. Our knowledge of the Johnsons' experiences in Maryland comes from Ross M. Kimmel's fine essay, "Free Blacks in Seventeenth-Century Maryland," *Maryland Historical Magazine*, LXXI (1976), 19–25. Also see, "Anthony Johnson, Free Negro, 1622," *Journal of Negro History*, LVI (1971), 71–75.

45. Whitelaw, *Virginia's Eastern Shore*, I, 671.

46. Kimmel, "Free Blacks," 24.

47. Ames, *Eastern Shore*, 25, 28, 30, 141.

48. Kimmel, "Free Blacks," 23–24. Kimmel argues that the Johnsons served as "retainers" to Toft and Revell.

49. *Ibid.*, 23.

50. *Ibid.*, 23–24.

51. *Ibid.*, 25.

52. See, Sidney W. Mintz and Richard Price, *An Anthropological Approach to the Afro-American Past: A Caribbean Perspective*, ISHI Occasional Papers in Social Change, No. 2 (Philadelphia, 1976), 1–21.

2 RACE RELATIONS AS STATUS AND PROCESS

1. See, Winthrop D. Jordan, "Modern Tensions and the Origins of American Slavery," *The Journal of Southern History*, XXVIII (1962), 18–30.

2. Kingsbury, ed., *Records of the Virginia Company*, III, 243. Also, Wesley Frank Craven, *White, Red, and Black: The Seventeenth-Century Virginian* (Charlottesville, 1971), 73–103.

3. One can find an example of this confusion in a letter written by a certain Mr. Moray in February 1665. Moray, a loyal Scot, explained that Virginia contained many of his countrymen, who "living better then ever ther forfathers, and that from so mean a beginning as being sold *slavs* here, after Hamiltons engagment and Worster fight are now herein great masters of many *servants* themselves . . ." ("Letters Written by Mr. Moray," *W&MQ*, 2nd Ser., II (1922), 160 (emphasis added)).

4. Oscar and Mary Handlin, "Origins of the Southern Labor System," *ibid.*, 3rd Ser., VII (1950), 199–222.

5. Carl N. Degler, "Slavery and the Genesis of American Race Prejudice," *Comparative Studies in Society and History*, II (1959), 52.

6. Jordan, "Modern Tensions," 20. Also see, Peter H. Wood, " 'I Did the Best I Could for My Day': The Study of Early Black History During the Second Reconstruction, 1960 to 1976," *W&MQ*, 3rd Ser., XXXV (1978), 206–210.

7. Jordan, "Modern Tensions," 22, 29. Also, *White Over Black*, 71–82.

8. Craven, *White, Red, and Black*, 76.

9. A. Leon Higginbotham, Jr., *In the Matter of Color: Race and the American Legal Process: The Colonial Period* (New York, 1978), 14.

10. William J. Wilson, *The Declining Significance of Race: Blacks and Changing American Institutions* (Chicago, 1978), x.

11. Fredrickson, "Toward a Social Interpretation . . . of American Racism," 242–243.

12. Herbert G. Gutman, *The Black Family in Slavery and Freedom, 1750–1925* (New York, 1976), 335.

13. Jordan, *White Over Black*, 588. Jordan's argument on the use of statutes is enthusiastically endorsed by Higginbotham in *Matter of Color*, 7–8.

14. See, T. H. Breen, "A Changing Labor Force and Race Relations in Virginia 1660–1710," *Journal of Social History*, VII (1973), 3–25. This discussion raises the complex problem of gentry hegemony. To what degree did a planter elite set the cultural standards for less affluent whites? To answer this question adequately would take us far beyond the temporal limits of this book. We are convinced, however, that the strength of planter hegemony varied throughout the colonial period. Before 1680 a group of wealthy families had not achieved undisputed dominance over the institu-

tional structure of the colony. There were successful men in Virginia, to be sure, but often these people died young or returned to England. Only after this date were certain major families in a position not only to secure economic and political power but also to pass it on to their children. Moreover, the sudden expansion of the black population at the end of the eighteenth century helped to create a sense of white solidarity that had not been present before Bacon's Rebellion. These demographic changes coupled with a long period of modest economic growth allowed gentry leaders to build beautiful mansions and courthouses, in other words, to create impressive stages on which to express competitive and individualistic values before an appreciative white audience. After 1750, gentry hegemony was seriously challenged, most dramatically by local religious dissenters. (See, Bernard Bailyn, "Politics and Social Structure in Virginia," in James Morton Smith, ed., *Seventeenth-Century America: Essays in Colonial History* (Chapel Hill, 1959), 90–115; John C. Rainbolt, "The Alteration in the Relationship Between Leadership and Constituents in Virginia, 1660 to 1720," *W&MQ*, 3rd Ser., XXVII (1970), 411–434; Edmund S. Morgan, "Slavery and Freedom: The American Paradox," *Journal of American History*, LIX (1972), 5–29; Rhys Isaac, "Evangelical Revolt: The Nature of the Baptists' Challenge to the Traditional Order in Virginia, 1765 to 1775," *W&MQ*, 3rd Ser., XXXI (1974), 345–343; T. H. Breen, "Horses and Gentlemen: The Cultural Significance of Gambling Among the Gentry of Virginia," *ibid.*, XXXIV (1977), 239–257.)

15. Morgan, "Slavery and Freedom," 21–22.
16. *W&MQ*, 2nd Ser., IV (1924), 147. A much abridged version of this law appeared in Hening, ed., *Statutes at Large*, I, 226.
17. Handlins, "Origins of the Southern Labor System," 199–222.
18. Degler, "Slavery and the Genesis of American Race Prejudice," 57.
19. Jordan, "Modern Tensions," 27.
20. Carl N. Degler, *Neither Black Nor White: Slavery and Race Relations in Brazil and the United States* (New York, 1971), 75–81.
21. *W&MQ*, 2nd Ser., IV (1924), 147.
22. NHCR, Order Book, 1674–1679, fol. 58.
23. Captain Thomas Grantham's "Account of My Transactions," Coventry Papers, LXXVII, fo. 301 (microfilm, Library of Congress); Charles M. Andrews, ed., *Narratives of the Insurrections, 1675–1690* (New York, 1915), 92–96; Wilcomb E. Washburn, *The Governor and the Rebel: A History of Bacon's Rebellion in Virginia* (Chapel Hill, 1957), 87–89; Thomas Grantham, *An Historical Account of Some Memorial Actions . . .* [London, 1716], ed., R. A. Brock (Richmond, 1882).
24. See, Breen, "Changing Labor Force," n. 63, 22.
25. Hening, ed., *Statutes at Large*, II, 481.

26. *Ibid.*, V, 17.
27. See, H. R. McIlwaine, ed., *Minutes of the Council and General Court* (Richmond, 1924), 467–468; Hening, ed., *Statutes at Large*, I, 254–255, 401, 440, 517–518; II, 21, 266, 273–274, 277–278, 299.
28. Degler, "Slavery and the Genesis of Race Prejudice," 58; Jordan, "Modern Tensions," 23–24.
29. McIlwaine, ed., *Minutes of Council*, 466.
30. Degler, "Slavery and the Genesis of Race Prejudice," 58.
31. Jordan, "Modern Tensions," 23–24.
32. McIlwaine, ed., *Minutes of Council*, 467.
33. Degler, "Slavery and the Genesis of Race Prejudice," 58.
34. McIlwaine, ed., *Minutes of Council*, 467.
35. Hening, ed., *Statutes at Large*, II, 26, 117.
36. *Ibid.*, 35, 299.
37. In *White Over Black*, Jordan suggests that the black man in the two 1640 cases was "possibly the same enterprising fellow" (75). The records, however, specifically name two different persons, and there appears to have been no connection between the two cases.
38. Winthrop D. Jordan provides a full analysis of the racial terminology employed by English planters in the mainland colonies in "American Chiaroscuro: The Status and Definition of Mulattoes in the British Colonies," *W&MQ*, 3rd Ser., XIX (1962), 183–220.
39. John Rex provides an excellent discussion of the problems of defining and interpreting what he calls a "race relations situation" in his *Race Relations in Sociological Theory* (London, 1970). Very important in helping us to understand the "interactionist" model were Fredrik Barth's "Introduction" to *Ethnic Groups and Boundaries: The Social Organization of Cultural Difference* (Boston, 1969), 9–38; Fredrik Barth, "Economic Spheres in Darfur," in Raymond Firth, ed., *Themes in Economic Anthropology* (London, 1967); Norman Long, *An Introduction to the Sociology of Rural Development* (London, 1977), 119–20; Gerald D. Berreman, "Scale and Social Relations," *Current Anthropology*, XIX (1978), 225–237; Thomas Bender, *Community and Social Change in America* (New Brunswick, N.J., 1978), 122–128.
40. *Models of Social Organization*, Royal Anthropological Institute, Occasional Papers, No. 23 (1966), 3; also, Erving Goffman, *The Presentation of Self in Everyday Life* (Edinburgh, 1958).
41. Eric R. Wolf, "Kinship, Friendship, and Patron-Client Relations in Complex Societies," in Michael Banton, ed., *The Social Anthropology of Complex Societies*, A.S.A. Monographs 4 (London, 1966), 16–17; John Duncan Powell, "Peasant Society and Clientelist Politics," *American Political Science Review*, LXIV (1970), 411–425.

42. Robert R. Kaufman, "The Patron-Client Concept and Macro-Politics: Prospects and Problems," *Comparative Studies in Society and History*, XVI (1974), 284–308.

43. Mintz and Price, *Anthropological Approach to the Afro-American Past*.

44. Barth wrote extensively about "sectors as spheres of exchange" in his paper *Models of Social Organization*. He developed the concept in order to analyze economic exchanges, but he seemed prepared to extend it to include other types of interaction. "We may adopt this view [the concept of separate spheres of activity]," Barth explained, "not only on what we conventionally regard as 'economic' exchanges, but look at all the prestations that circulate in a society in terms of what are their appropriate reciprocals, and thus observe the resultant patterns by which value in its different forms flows. Just as yams and *kula* objects in the Trobriands belong in different market spheres and thus flow in different circuits, so one might say in our society that political prestations, though they imply reciprocity, belong to a different sphere from that of sex, or from that in which money circulates, and cannot legitimately be reciprocated for in such forms of value" (17).

3   NORTHAMPTON COUNTY AT MID-CENTURY

1. Two excellent studies of the ecology of the Eastern Shore are William W. Warner, *Beautiful Swimmers: Watermen, Crabs and the Chesapeake Bay* (Boston, 1976) and Boyd Gibbons, *Wye Island* (Baltimore, 1977). We appreciate Brooks Miles Barnes's willingness to share with us his "A Selected, Annotated Bibliography of the Eastern Shore of Virginia for the Colonial Period" (unpublished Master's thesis, University of North Carolina, 1977). This is the fullest guide to the literature on Virginia's Eastern Shore available.

2. *A Perfect Description of Virginia . . .* , in Force, comp., *Tracts*, II, No. 8, 7. See, J. H. Hexter, "Storm Over the Gentry," in his *Reappraisals in History* (New York, 1963), 117–149.

3. Colonel [Henry] Norwood, *A Voyage to Virginia* [London, 1649], in Force, comp., *Tracts*, III, No. 10, 28-29. Fortunately for Norwood, he had read Captain John Smith's description of Virginia. When Norwood reached the mainland, he found himself confronted with a group of Eastern Shore Indians. After fumbling for a way to communicate with these people, "it came at last into my head, that I had long since read Mr. [John] *Smith's* travels thro' those parts of *America*, and that the word *Werowance* . . . was in *English* the king" (30).

4. Jennings C. Wise in his anecdotal local history, *Kingdome of Accawmacke*, provides a "Translation of Certain Indian Names," but we have no way to verify the authenticity of Wise's claims. For what it is worth, he believed

that Pungoteague meant "sand-fly river" (371). Another antiquarian historian reported "Tradition tells us that a canoe load of pioneers crossed the great Chesapioque from Jamestown soon after Captain Smith's discovery; intermarried with the tribe of Nassawattox, and were found enjoying semi-civilization and savagery when the tide of immigration trended eastward in 1615" (*VMHB*, V (1897), 128).

5. Smith, *Travels and Works*, II, 413.
6. Cited in Wise, *Kingdome of Accawmacke*, 21.
7. See, Arthur Pierce Middleton, *Tobacco Coast: A Maritime History of Chesapeake Bay in the Colonial Era* (Newport, Virginia, 1953), 33.
8. CCR, *1640–1645*, 26–27.
9. H. R. McIlwaine, ed., *Journals of the House Burgesses of Virginia 1659/60–1693* (Richmond, 1914), 101.
10. Charles B. Clark, ed., *The Eastern Shore of Maryland and Virginia* (3 vols., New York, 1950), I, 30–33; Smith, *Travels and Works*, II, 413.
11. *Climatic Atlas of the United States* (Washington, D.C., 1968), 1–23.
12. Smith, *Travels and Works*, II, 413; Clark, ed., *Eastern Shore*, I, 34–35; *The National Atlas of the United States of America* (Washington, D.C., 1970), 75, 78–79.
13. Norwood, *A Voyage to Virginia*, 48.
14. *National Atlas*, 97; Laing, "Cattle in Seventeenth-Century Virginia," 146.
15. CCR, *1640–1645*, 272–273, 441; *National Atlas*, 90–91.
16. Norwood, *Voyage to Virginia*, 36–48.
17. Morgan, *American Slavery—American Freedom*, 415.
18. Ames, *Eastern Shore*, 51–53.
19. *Calendar of State Papers, America and West Indies, 1693–96*, 519.
20. Smith, *Travels and Works*, II, 569.
21. Ames, *Eastern Shore*, 7–8.
22. Norwood, *Voyage to Virginia*, 45; CCR, *1632–1640*, xx.
23. *Journal of Jasper Danckaerts, 1679–1680*, eds. B. James and J. Franklin Jameson (New York, 1913), 120. See, Earle, *The Evolution of a Tidewater Settlement System*, 142–169.
24. NHCR, Order Book, No. 9, 1664–1674, fol. 9; Wise, *Kingdome of Accawmacke*, 291–292.
25. CCR, 1632–1640, 54.
26. Wise, *Kingdome of Accawmacke*, 291–292.
27. CCR, *1632–1640*, xlv.
28. CCR, *1640–1645*, 182, 188, 327, 355, 386, 455.
29. Smith, *Travels and Works*, II, 413.
30. McIlwaine, ed., *Minutes of the Council*, 445.
31. Smith, *Travels and Works*, II, 570.
32. Ames, *Eastern Shore*, 4–5. The most useful general account of this trou-

bled period of Virginia history is Craven, *Southern Colonies in the Seventeenth Century*, 93–137.

33. Morgan, *American Slavery—American Freedom*, 105–130.

34. Ames, *Eastern Shore*, 20.

35. The best analysis of these complex changes is Susie M. Ames, "The Reunion of Two Virginia Counties," *Journal of Southern History*, VIII (1942), 536–548.

36. Cited, *ibid.*, 537.

37. Ames, *Eastern Shore*, 45–47.

38. Lyon G. Tyler, "Virginia Under the Commonwealth," W&MQ, 1st Ser., I (1892–93), 191; Craven, *Southern Colonies in the Seventeenth Century*, 293.

39. Hening, ed., *Statutes at Large*, I, 396, 520.

40. A *Perfect Description*, in Force, comp., *Tracts*, II, No. 8, 7.

41. Edmund S. Morgan provides a thorough discussion of Northampton's demographic structure in *American Slavery—American Freedom*, 395–432. For an analysis of the character and distribution of the Eastern Shore population in the 1620s see, W. E. Wilkins, Jr., "The Population of the Eastern Shore in 1623/4 and 1624/5," *Studies and Research* [Madison College Bulletin], XXXIV (1975), 5–20. We thank Brooks Miles Barnes for bringing this article to our attention.

42. Hening, ed., *Statutes at Large*, II, 515.

43. *Journal of Jasper Danckaerts*, 151. See, Darrett B. and Anita H. Rutman, "Of Agues and Fevers: Malaria in the Early Chesapeake," W&MQ, 3rd Ser., XXXIII (1976), 31–60; Curtin, "Epidemiology and the Slave Trade," 190-216.

44. Carr and Walsh, "The Planter's Wife," 532–571; Russell R. Menard, "Immigrants and Their Increase: The Process of Population Growth in Early Colonial Maryland," in Aubrey Land et al., eds., *Law, Society, and Politics in Early Maryland* (Baltimore, 1977), 88–110.

45. Hening, ed., *Statutes at Large*, II, 541.

46. One could argue that our seven-part system is unnecessarily complex and that Englishmen of this period recognized the existence of only two groups, gentlemen, comprising at most 5 percent of English society, and the rest, average men and women, some modestly well-to-do, others quite poor. According to Lawrence Stone, "The most fundamental dichotomy within the [English] society was between the gentleman and the non-gentleman, a division that was based essentially upon the distinction between those who did, and those who did not, have to work with their hands" ("Social Mobility in England, 1500–1700," *Past and Present*, No. 33 (1966), 17, 18–20). And Peter Laslett states, "If you were not a gentleman, if you were not ordinarily called 'Master' by the commoner folk, or 'Your Worship'; if you, like

nearly all the rest, had a Christian and a surname and nothing more; then you counted for little in the world outside your own household, and for almost nothing outside your small village community and its neighbourhood" (*The World We Have Lost: England Before the Industrial Age* (New York, 1965), 26, see chap. II, "A One-Class Society," 22–52). The problem with this model is that it was developed to describe English society—really the English political structure—and colonial Virginia was not England. We found it helpful, therefore, to include separate racial groups, especially when many blacks were slaves for life, as well as a large number of servants who powerfully shaped the character of daily affairs in Northampton in ways that their counterparts in England did not. We agree, however, that within the *free white* population of the Eastern Shore there were only two important categories, the great planters (the gentry) and the small planters.

47. George B. Curtis, "The Colonial County Court, Social Forum and Legislative Precedent: Accomack County, Virginia, 1633–1639," *VMHB*, LXXXV (1977), 274–280.
48. William Bullock, *Virginia Impartially Examined, and Left to Publick View* . . . (London, 1649), 3.
49. See, Bailyn, "Politics and Social Structure," 94–98.
50. Susie M. Ames, "Colonel Edmund Scarborough," *Alumnae Bulletin of Randolph-Macon Woman's College*, No. 26, 17.
51. *CCR, 1640–1645*, 54–55.
52. *Ibid.*, 55–56, 83, 153, 272–273, 278–279; Ames, *Eastern Shore*, 22–25.
53. *CCR, 1640–1645*, 154–155, 231–232; Ames, *Eastern Shore*, 109–122, 132–138.
54. John Spencer Bassett, "The Relation Between the Virginia Planter and the London Merchant," *Annual Report of the American Historical Association for the Year 1901* (Washington, D.C., 1902), 556–563; Morgan, *American Slavery—American Freedom*, 224; Sister Joan de Lourdes Leonard, "Operation Checkmate: The Birth and Death of a Virginia Blueprint for Progress, 1660–1676," *W&MQ*, 3rd Ser., XXIV (1967), 44–74.
55. Byrd to Charles Boyle, Earl of Orrery, July 5, 1726, in Marion Tinling, ed., *The Correspondence of the Three William Byrds of Westover, Virginia, 1684–1776* (2 vols., Charlottesville, 1977), I, 355.
56. See, Gerald W. Mullin, *Flight and Rebellion: Slave Resistance in Eighteenth-Century Virginia* (New York, 1972), intro. and chap. I.
57. See, Breen, "Horses and Gentlemen," 238–257; Isaac, "Evangelical Revolt," 345–353.
58. Morgan, *American Slavery—American Freedom*, 148, 195; Warren M. Billings, "The Growth of Political Institutions in Virginia, 1634 to 1676," *W&MQ*, 3rd Ser., XXXI (1974), 226.

59. Cited in Ames, *Eastern Shore*, 72.

60. See, Breen, "Changing Labor Force"; Russell Menard, "From Servants to Slaves: The Transformation of the Chesapeake Labor System," *Southern Studies*, XVI (1977), 360–368.

61. Sidney W. Mintz, "The Origins of Reconstituted Peasantries," in *Caribbean Transformations* (Chicago, 1974), 150–151.

62. Ames, *Eastern Shore*, 87.

63. *Ibid*.

64. *Ibid*.

65. Records quoted in *ibid*., 19; Ames, "Colonel Edmund Scarborough," 18–19.

66. "Northampton County Records in the 17th Century," *VMHB*, V (1897), 33. Scarborough seems to have been able to raise a body of armed men whenever he pleased (see, Ames, "Colonel Edmund Scarborough," 19; Ames, "Reunion of Two Counties," 540; "Colonel Scarborough's Report: Being An Account of His Efforts to Suppress the Quakers In What Is Now Part of Maryland, Then Claimed By Virginia," *VMHB*, XIX (1911), 173). His extraordinary behavior reminds one of the activities of "over-mighty subjects" during the late Tudor period. Compare, for example, the English cases described in W. H. Dunham, "Lord Hastings' Indentured Retainers, 1461–1483: The Lawfulness of Livery and Retaining Under the Yorkists and Tudors," *Transactions of the Connecticut Academy of Arts and Sciences*, XXX (1955), 1–175.

67. Ames, "Colonel Edmund Scarborough," 23.

68. See, Wise, *Kingdome of Accawmacke*, 124–152.

69. Ames, "Reunion of Two Counties," 536–548; Warren M. Billings, " 'Virginia's Deploured Condition,' 1660–1676: The Coming of Bacon's Rebellion" (Ph.D. diss., Northern Illinois University, 1968), 71–73.

70. McIlwaine, ed., *Journals of the House of Burgesses*, 99, also 91.

71. CCR, *1640–1645*, 214; for more information on Pope's life, particularly his brushes with the law, see, CCR, *1632–1640*, 108, 129, 139, 151.

72. CCR, *1640–1645*, 218, 392. For valuable discussions of the distribution of wealth in colonial Chesapeake society see, Aubrey C. Land, "Economic Base and Social Structure: The Northern Chesapeake in the Eighteenth Century," *Journal of Economic History*, XXV (1965), 139–154; Russell R. Menard, "From Servant to Freeholder: Status Mobility and Property Accumulation in Seventeenth-Century Maryland," *W&MQ*, 3rd Ser., XXX (1973), 37–64; Russell R. Menard, P. M. G. Harris, and Lois Green Carr, "Opportunity and Inequality: The Distribution of Wealth on the Lower Western Shore of Maryland, 1638–1705," *Maryland Historical Magazine*, LXIX (1974), 169–184. The authors of this last essay argue that "Maryland was a good poor man's country in the middle decades of the seventeenth

century. . . . There were, of course, still indentured servants, free laborers, tenants, and sharecroppers in Maryland as well as men who were
much wealthier than their neighbors. However, the small, owner-operated
plantation had emerged as the dominant feature on the landscape" (182).
To what degree these Maryland findings are applicable to Virginia is not yet
certain. Considering the sad condition of most county records from this
period, we may never be able to compare the social structures of these two
colonies with precision. Nevertheless, it is clear that the number of small
planters in Virginia was increasing during the middle decades of the seventeenth century. To describe Virginia at this time as a good poor man's
country would be misleading, however, for whatever the value of the
Virginians' estates may have been, many small planters believed themselves
economically oppressed and complained about their poverty. See, Morgan,
American Slavery—American Freedom, 215–234 and Breen, "Changing
Labor Force," 3–11.

73. CCR, *1632–1640*, 27, 66.
74. CCR, *1640–1645*, 97–98.
75. *Ibid.*, 395. One small home, Pear Valley, built in 1672 survives, but it is
    in an advanced state of disrepair (see, H. Chandlee Forman, *The Virginia
    Eastern Shore and Its British Origins* (Easton, Md., 1975), 48–55).
76. Morgan, *American Slavery—American Freedom*, 425.
77. Craven, *White, Red, and Black*, 5–9.
78. It is possible, of course, that local geography in other parts of Virginia
    proved more conducive to the development of group identities. In some
    counties, notably York and Gloucester in the early 1660s, small planters
    seem to have joined with indentured servants to protest their common pov-
    erty. No risings of this type occurred on the Eastern Shore. See, Breen,
    "Changing Labor Force," 7–9.
79. This point is developed more fully for another society by Sutti R. De Ortiz
    in *Uncertainties in Peasant Farming: A Colombian Case* (New York,
    1973), 1–20 and *passim*.
80. CCR, *1640–1645*, 30–32, 121.
81. Philip A. Bruce, *Institutional History of Virginia in the Seventeenth Cen-
    tury* (2 vols., Gloucester, Mass., 1964), I, 33.
82. Cited in Alan Everitt, *The Community of Kent and the Great Rebellion,
    1640–60* (Leicester, 1966), 318.
83. Joan Thirsk, ed., *The Agrarian History of England and Wales, 1500–1640*
    (Cambridge, Eng., 1967), 458.
84. On several occasions during the seventeenth century the House of
    Burgesses attempted to legislate official holidays. Two of these commemo-
    rated the massacre of Virginia settlers by local Indian tribes and one cele-
    brated the exposure of a plot on the part of disaffected indentured servants

to overthrow the Virginia gentry. For reasons not too difficult to understand none of these holidays became popular, and after a few efforts to spark interest in these special days failed, the colonial legislature allowed the memory of massacres and servant plots to fade away. Hening, ed., *Statutes at Large*, I, 123, 177, 202, 263, 290, 459; II, 191, 204; Robert Beverley, *The History and Present State of Virginia*, ed. by Louis B. Wright (Chapel Hill, 1947), 69–70.

85. See, Edmund S. Morgan, "The First American Boom: Virginia 1618 to 1630," *W&MQ*, 3rd Ser., XXVIII (1971), 182.

86. The contrast between New England and Virginia is striking. People generally moved to Massachusetts Bay within stable nuclear families. See, T. H. Breen and Stephen Foster, "Moving to the New World: The Character of Early Massachusetts Immigration," *W&MQ*, 3rd Ser., XXX (1973), 189–222. Nor is there substantial evidence that men and women came to the Chesapeake region during this period as part of a chain migration. For a recent discussion of this form of settlement see, Josef J. Barton, *Peasants and Strangers: Italians, Rumanians, and Slovaks in an American City, 1890–1950* (Cambridge, Mass., 1975), 48–63.

87. Julian Pitt-Rivers presents a useful analysis of the cultural problems created by strangers in *The Fate of Shechem, or the Politics of Sex: Essays in the Anthropology of the Mediterranean* (Cambridge, Eng., 1977), 94–112.

88. William Hubbard, *The Happiness of a People in the Wisdome of their Rulers Directing and in the Obedience of their Brethren Attending Unto what Israel ought to do* (Boston, 1676), 9–10.

89. The literature on patterns of literacy in seventeenth-century Virginia is quite limited, but Kenneth A. Lockridge makes some interesting suggestions on this topic in *Literacy in Colonial New England: An Enquiry into the Social Context of Literacy in the Early Modern West* (New York, 1974), 4, 73–87.

90. See, Morgan, *American Slavery—American Freedom*, 248–249.

91. *CCR, 1640–1645*, 238.

92. *Ibid.*, 313.

93. *Ibid.*, 351.

94. *Ibid.*, 118–119.

95. Craven, *White, Red, and Black*, 5.

96. There are no surviving tithable lists for Northampton County before 1664, and thus, for much of our period of study we possess no information on household structure. After that date, however, it is possible to supplement scattered pieces of information about servant life with rough statistics. According to Edmund Morgan, 1,043 persons were mentioned by name on the extant tithable lists 1664 to 1677. Of these persons, "578 appear only as non-householders." Since a great majority of those non-householders were

servants, we obtain a general sense of the large size of the servant population. However, many other people in Northampton during this period worked as servants, perhaps completing indentures, before rising to the level of householder (see, Morgan, *American Slavery—American Freedom*, 423–432).

97. See, E. A. Wrigley, "London's Importance 1650–1750," *Past and Present*, No. 37 (1967), 44–70; Breen and Foster, "Moving to the New World," 189–222.
98. The quotation is found in Peter Wilson Coldham, "The 'Spiriting' of London Children to Virginia, 1648–1685," *VMHB*, LXXXIII (1975), 283.
99. Bullock, *Virginia Impartially Examined*, 2–8, 14; Hammond, *Leah and Rachel*, 12–19.
100. Cited in A. E. Smith, *Colonists in Bondage: White Servitude and Convict Labor in America, 1607–1776* (New York, 1971), 70.
101. Craven, *White, Red, and Black*, 7. See, [Anonymous], *The Vain Prodigal Life, and Tragical Penitent Death of Thomas Hellier* . . . (London, 1680), 5–40.
102. Bullock, *Virginia Impartially Examined*, 14.
103. Hammond, *Leah and Rachel*, 11.
104. Hening, ed., *Statutes at Large*, I, 257, 441; II, 113, 169, 240.
105. *Ibid.*, II, 118.
106. CCR, *1640–1645*, 184, 453.
107. For a discussion of the problems of using this type of data see, Morgan, "Headrights and Head Counts," 361–371.
108. CCR, *1640–1645*, 279–280.
109. See, Smith, *Colonists in Bondage*, chap. I.
110. Mildred Campbell, "Social Origins of Some Early Americans," in Smith, ed., *Seventeenth-Century America*, 63–89; David W. Galenson, " 'Middling People' or 'Common Sort'?: The Social Origins of Some Early Americans Reexamined," *W&MQ*, 3rd Ser., XXXV (1978), 499–522.
111. Lorena S. Walsh, "Servitude and Opportunity in Charles County, Maryland, 1658–1705," in Land et al., eds., *Law, Society, and Politics*, III; Carr and Walsh, "The Planter's Wife," 542–571; Galenson, " 'Middling People,' " 522.
112. Craven, *White, Red, and Black*, 5.
113. Hening, ed., *Statutes at Large*, I, 254–255, 440; II, 118.
114. Ames, *Eastern Shore*, 86–87.
115. CCR, *1640–1645*, 22, 26.
116. *Ibid.*, 22–26.
117. Hening, ed., *Statutes at Large*, II, 167.
118. *Ibid.*, 113–118, 195.
119. *Ibid.*, 273–274.

120. *Ibid.*, 119, 195, 273, 277–278.
121. *Ibid.*, 273–274 (emphasis added).
122. See, Douglas Hay, "Property, Authority and the Criminal Law," in Hay et al., eds., *Albion's Fatal Tree: Crime and Society in Eighteenth-Century England* (New York, 1975), 17–66.
123. CCR, *1640–1645*, 212.
124. *Ibid.*, 276.
125. CCR, *1632–1640*, 120–121.
126. *Ibid.*, 120; CCR, *1640–1645*, 459.

4 THE FREE BLACKS OF THE EASTERN SHORE

1. Morgan, *American Slavery—American Freedom*, 420–432.
2. Morgan, "Slavery and Freedom," 18, n. 39.
3. Frederickson, "A Social Interpretation . . . of American Racism," 247.
4. See, Sidney Mintz, "History and Anthropology: A Brief Reprise," in Stanley L. Engerman and Eugene D. Genovese, eds., *Race and Slavery in the Western Hemisphere: Quantitative Studies* (Princeton, 1975), 477–494.
5. Edmund Jennings to the Board of Trade, 27 November 1708, in Elizabeth Donnan, ed., *Documents Illustrative of the History of the Slave Trade to America* (4 vols., Washington, D.C., 1930–35), IV, 89.
6. K. G. Davies, *The Royal African Company* (London, 1957), 38–44; Morgan, *American Slavery—American Freedom*, 299–302.
7. Curtin, "Epidemiology and the Slave Trade," 196–210.
8. Morgan Godwyn, *The Negro's and Indian's Advocate* (London, 1680), 101; also see, Richard Ligon, *A True and Exact History of Barbados (London, 1673)*, 43–47.
9. See, C. R. Boxer, *The Dutch Seaborne Empire: 1600–1800* (New York, 1965), 238–239; C. R. Boxer, *The Portuguese Seaborne Empire: 1415–1825* (London, 1969), 96–112; Miller, "Congo-Angola Slave Trade," 76–113. A few Angolans came to Virginia by a more direct avenue. In 1628 a Captain Guy or Gay captured a vessel off Angola containing slaves, and he sold these people in Virginia for tobacco (Vaughan, "Blacks, in Virginia: A Note on the First Decade," 477). One Virginia slave even produced written proof of Portuguese contact, but unfortunately it did him little good. In 1667 Fernando, a slave living in Lower Norfolk, sued for freedom in a county court, protesting that he was a Christian and offering in support of his claims certain papers "in Portugell or some other language which the Court could not understand" (Warren M. Billings, "The Case of Fernando and Elizabeth Key: A Note on the Status of Blacks in Seventeenth-Century Virginia," *W&MQ*, 3rd Ser., XXX (1973), 467–468).
10. Ames, *Eastern Shore*, 47–49; Craven, *White, Red, and Black*, 91; also Bruce, *Economic History*, II, 300–316.

11. Boxer, *Portuguese Seaborne Empire*, 96–103; Miller, "Congo-Angola Slave Trade," 76–113; David Birmingham, *Trade and Conflict in Angola: The Mbundu and Their Neighbors under the Influence of the Portuguese, 1483–1790* (Oxford, 1966).

12. See, Edmund S. Morgan, "The Labor Problem at Jamestown, 1607–1618," *American Historical Review*, LXXVI (1971), 595–611.

13. Michael Kammen, *Colonial New York: A History* (New York, 1975), 58–59; Ellis Lawrence Raesly, *Portrait of New Netherland* (New York, 1945), 162; *New York Times*, December 7, 1977, 41.

14. Morgan, *American Slavery—American Freedom*, 154.

15. Hammond, *Leah and Rachel*, 14 (emphasis added).

16. NHCR, Order Book, No. VIII, 1657–1664, fol. 107–108; Deeds, Wills, Nos. 7, 8, 1654–1668, fol. 32.

17. NHCR, Deeds, Wills, Etc., No. 4, 1651–1654, fol. 119.

18. *Ibid.*

19. *Ibid.*

20. *Ibid.*

21. Morgan, *American Slavery—American Freedom*, 175–176.

22. NHCR, Deeds, Wills, Nos. 7, 8, 1654–1668, fol. 19, 20.

23. It is unclear exactly when or how Driggus obtained freedom. At the time he negotiated with Pott for his children's freedom he seems to have been a slave. By the 1660s, however, Driggus was listed among the tithables as an independent head of household.

24. Ames, *Eastern Shore*, 97.

25. NHCR, Deeds, Wills, Etc., No. 3, 1645–1651, fol. 82.

26. NHCR, Deeds, Wills, Etc., No. 4, 1651–1654, fol. 92; Ames, *Eastern Shore*, 96–97.

27. NHCR, Deeds, Wills, Nos. 7, 8, 1654–1668, fol. 74.

28. *Ibid.*, pt. II, fol. 8.

29. Morgan, *American Slavery—American Freedom*, 142, 198, 204.

30. NHCR, Deeds, Wills, Etc., 1657–1666, fol. 70, 74.

31. NHCR, Deeds, Wills, Etc., No. 5, 1654–1655, fol. 54.

32. *Ibid.*

33. NHCR, Deeds, Wills, Etc., No. 4, 1651–1654, fol. 178.

34. NHCR, Deeds, Wills, Etc., No. 3, 1645–1651, fol. 217.

35. *CCR, 1640–1645*, 32.

36. NHCR, Deeds, Wills, Etc., no. 3, 1645–1651, fol. 150.

37. *Ibid.*

38. *Ibid.*, fol. 152.

39. Mintz, *Caribbean Transformations*, 155.

40. NHCR, Deeds, Etc., 1668–1680, fol. 3; Ames, *Eastern Shore*, 106.

41. NHCR, Deeds, Etc., 1668–1680, fol. 34, 43.

42. NHCR, Deeds, Wills, Nos. 7, 8, 1654–1668, fol. 12.

43. Whitelaw, *Virginia's Eastern Shore*, I, 228; II, 1216.

44. Brewer, "Negro Property Owners," 576–577; Whitelaw, *Virginia's Eastern Shore*, I, 206, 228; II, 1216.

45. Earle, *The Evolution of a Tidewater Settlement*, 27.

46. NHCR, Order Book, No. 9, 1664–1674, fol. 160; Deeds, Wills, Nos. 7, 8, 1654–1668, fol. 21; Order Book, 1674–1679, fol. 15.

47. Morgan, *American Slavery—American Freedom*, 136–140.

48. NHCR, Deeds, Wills, Etc., No. 4, 1651–1654, fol. 114.

49. NHCR, Deeds, Wills, Etc., 1657–1666, fol. 60, 106, 161; also Deeds, Wills, Etc., No. 4, 1651–1654, fol. 114.

50. NHCR, Deeds, Wills, Nos. 7, 8, 1654–1668, fol. 19; Deeds, Wills, Etc., 1657–1666, fol. 74.

51. NHCR, Order Book, 1674–1679, fol. 273.

52. NHCR, Deeds, Wills, Etc., No. 3, 1645–1651, fol. 55; Deeds, Wills, Etc., No. 4, 1651–1654, fol. 123; Deeds, Wills, Etc., No. 5, 1654–1655, fol. 38.

53. See, Allan Kulikoff, "The Beginnings of the Afro-American Family in Maryland," in Land et al., eds., *Law, Society, and Politics in Early Maryland*, 172–174.

54. Morgan, *American Slavery—American Freedom*, 430.

55. *Ibid.*, 334; Ames, *Eastern Shore*, 96–97; NHCR, Deeds, Etc., 1668–1680, fol. 3; Order Book, No. 9, 1664–1674, fol. 221.

56. NHCR, Deeds, Wills, Nos. 7, 8, 1654–1668, pt. II, fol. 12 [emphasis added]; Ralph Wormeley, a self-styled "gentleman" from York County, recorded a similar, though more elaborate, agreement in 1645 (*CCR, 1640–1645*, 433–434).

57. NHCR, Deeds, Etc., 1668–1680, fol. 60.

58. *Ibid.*, fol. 59, 60.

59. Accomack County Records, Order Book, 1666–1670, fol. 152, 154.

60. NHCR, Order Book, No. 9, 1664–1674, fol. 221.

61. *Ibid.*, fol. 89.

62. See, Sidney W. Mintz and Eric R. Wolf, "An Analysis of Ritual Coparenthood (Compadrazgo)," *Southwestern Journal of Anthropology*, VI (1950), 341–368; Sidney W. Mintz, "A Note on the Definition of Peasantries," *The Journal of Peasant Studies*, I (1973), 97.

63. Morgan, *American Slavery—American Freedom*, 240.

64. NHCR, Deeds, Wills, Etc., No. 4, 1651–1654, fol. 33.

65. NHCR, Order Book, No. VIII, 1657–1664, fol. 68, 183, 186.

66. Hening, ed., *Statutes at Large*, II, 215.

67. See, Mark De Wolfe Howe, "The Sources and Nature of Law in Colonial Massachusetts," in George Athan Billias, ed., *Selected Essays: Law and Authority in Colonial America* (Barre, Mass., 1965), 1–15.

68. NHCR, Deeds, Wills, Etc., No. 4, 1651–1654, fol. 38, 50.

69. NHCR, Order Book, No. 9, 1664–1674, fol. 131, 138, 139, 144.

70. *Ibid.*

71. NHCR, Deeds, Wills, Etc., No. 4, 1651–1654, fol. 200; Deeds, Wills, Etc., 1657–1666, fol. 57, 58.

72. *Ibid.*

73. NHCR, Order Book, No. VIII, 1657–1664, fol. 19.

74. NHCR, Deeds, Etc., 1668–1680, fol. 3.

75. NHCR, Deeds, Wills, Etc., No. 5, 1654–1655, fol. 54, 60; also, Morgan, *American Slavery—American Freedom,* 156–157.

76. NHCR, Deeds, Wills, Nos. 7, 8, 1654–1668, fol. 21.

77. NHCR, Order Book, No. VIII, 1657–1664, fol. 188.

78. *Ibid.*, fol. 32.

79. *Ibid.*, fol. 179.

80. NHCR, Order Book, No. 9, 1664–1674, fol. 35; see, Bruce, *Institutional History,* I, 45–50.

81. NHCR, Order Book, No. 9, 1664–1674, fol. 30.

82. *Ibid.*, fol. 33, 35.

83. *Ibid.*, fol. 254.

84. This phrase appeared in NHCR, Order Book, No. VIII, 1657–1664, fol. 25.

85. NHCR, Order Book, No. 9, 1664–1674, fol. 35.

86. Accomack, Deeds and Wills, 1663–1666, fol. 92, 100.

87. NHCR, Order Book, No. 9, 1664–1674, fol. 41–42.

88. Hening, ed., *Statutes at Large,* II, 281; see also Donald L. Noel, "A Theory of the Origin of Ethnic Stratification," *Social Problems,* XVI (1968), 158–172.

89. "Letters Written by Mr. Moray," 159–160.

90. NHCR, Deeds, Wills, Etc., No. 5, 1654–1655, fol. 100.

91. Cited in Russell, *Free Negro,* 27.

92. NHCR, Deeds, Wills, Nos. 7, 8, 1654–1668, fol. 21.

93. NHCR, Order Book, No. 9, 1664–1674 fol. 63.

94. NHCR, Order Book, No. VIII, 1657–1664, fol. 122.

95. NHCR, Order Book, 1674–1679, fol. 15.

96. NHCR, Deeds, Wills, Etc., 1657–1666, fol. 161.

97. *Ibid.*, fol. 17.

98. NHCR, Deeds, Wills, Etc., No. 3, 1645–1651, fol. 111a.

99. *Ibid.*, fol. 131.

100. Accomack County Records, Order Book, 1666–1670, fol. 161, 162.

101. NHCR, Deeds, Wills, Etc., 1657–1666, fol. 123; Ames, *Eastern Shore,* 107.

102. NHCR, Deeds, Wills, Etc., 1657–1666, fol. 74.

103. NHCR, Deeds, Etc., No. 5, 1654–1655, fol. 138–139.
104. NHCR, Order Book, No. 9, 1664–1674, fol. 29.
105. *Ibid.*, fol. 44.
106. NHCR, Order Book, No. 9, 1664–1674, fol. 156; Accomack County Records, Order Book, 1673–1676, fol. 31.
107. NHCR, Deeds, Wills, Nos. 7, 8, 1654–1668, pt. II, fol. 15.
108. NHCR, Order Book, No. 9, 1664–1674, fol. 89.
109. *Ibid.*, fol. 52.
110. *Ibid.*
111. See, for example, Richard Dunn, *Sugar and Slaves* (Chapel Hill, 1973), 250; Allan Kulikoff, "Black Society and the Economics of Slavery," *Maryland Historical Magazine*, LXX (1975), 207; Russell R. Menard, "The Maryland Slave Population, 1658 to 1730: A Demographic Profile of Blacks in Four Counties," *W&MQ*, 3rd Ser., XXXII (1975), 53–54.
112. NHCR, Deeds, Wills, Nos. 7, 8, 1654–1668, pt. II, fol. 17.
113. NHCR, Order Book, 1674–1679, fol. 12, 19.
114. NHCR, Order Book, No. 9, 1664–1674 fol. 54–55.
115. *CCR, 1640–1645*, 84.
116. NHCR, Order Book, 1674–1679, fol. 95; Order Book, No. VIII, 1657–1664, fol. 68.
117. NHCR, Order Book, No. 9, 1664–1674, fol. 31.
118. *Ibid.*
119. NHCR, Order Book, No. VIII, 1657–1664, fol. 175.
120. See, Herbert S. Klein, *Slavery in the Americas: A Comparative Study of Virginia and Cuba* (Chicago, 1967), 227–235; Fredrickson, "Toward a Social Interpretation . . . of American Racism," 246–248.
121. Paul G. F. Clemens, "The Settlement and Growth of Maryland's Eastern Shore During the English Restoration," *Maryland Historian*, V (1974), 63–78.
122. Kimmel, "Free Blacks," 21.
123. This shift is analyzed in more detail in Breen, "A Changing Labor Force," 3–25; also see, Menard, "From Servants to Slaves," 355–390.
124. Hening, ed., *Statutes at Large*, II, 267.
125. *Ibid.*, III, 87–88.
126. Ames, *Eastern Shore*, 107–108.

5 CONCLUSION: PROPERTY AND THE CONTEXT OF FREEDOM

1. Morgan, *American Slavery—American Freedom*, 154–157.
2. Long, *Sociology of Rural Development*, 134.
3. Mintz, *Caribbean Transformations*, 141. For his provocative discussion of New World peasantries, see, 131–156.

4. Fredrik Barth, *Ethnic Groups and Boundaries*, 30–32.

5. The fullest account of these changes is Morgan, *American Slavery—American Freedom*, 215–292; also see, Thomas J. Wertenbaker, *The Planters of Colonial Virginia* (Princeton, 1922).

Index